JAICO PUBLISHING HOUSE
Elevate Your Life. Transform Your World.

Established in 1946, Jaico Publishing House is the publisher of stellar authors such as Sri Sri Paramahansa Yogananda, Osho, Robin Sharma, Deepak Chopra, Stephen Hawking, Eknath Easwaran, Sarvapalli Radhakrishnan, Nirad Chaudhuri, Khushwant Singh, Mulk Raj Anand, John Maxwell, Ken Blanchard and Brian Tracy. Our list which has crossed a landmark 2000 titles, is amongst the most diverse in the country, with books in religion, spirituality, mind/body/spirit, self-help, business, cookery, humour, career, games, biographies, fiction, and science.

Jaico has expanded its horizons to become a leading publisher of educational and professional books in management and engineering. Our college-level textbooks and reference titles are used by students countrywide. The success of our academic and professional titles is largely due to the efforts of our Educational and Corporate Sales Divisions.

The late Mr. Jaman Shah established Jaico as a book distribution company. Sensing that independence was around the corner, he aptly named his company Jaico ("Jai" means victory in Hindi). In order to tap the significant demand for affordable books in a developing nation, Mr. Shah initiated Jaico's own publications. Jaico was India's first publisher of paperback books in the English language.

In addition to being a publisher and distributor of its own titles, Jaico is a major distributor of books of leading international publishers such as McGraw Hill, Pearson, Cengage Learning, John Wiley and Elsevier Science. With its headquarters in Mumbai, Jaico has other sales offices in Ahmedabad, Bangalore, Bhopal, Chennai, Delhi, Hyderabad and Kolkata. Our sales team of over 40 executives, direct mail order division, and website ensure that our books effectively reach all urban and rural parts of the country.

SINCE 1946

Bibliography

- Brown, Robert, ed. Ganesh: Studies of an Asian God. Delhi: Sri Satguru Publications, 1991.
- Coupe, Lawrence. Myth. London: Routledge, 1997.
- Courtright, Paul B. Ganesha: Lord of Obstacles, Lord of Beginning. Delhi: Motilal Banarsidass, 1985.
- Dange, Sadashiv Ambadas. Encyclopaedia of Puranic Beliefs and Practices, Vol. 1–5. New Delhi: Navrang, 1990.
- Danielou, Alain. Gods of Love and Ecstasy: The Traditions of Shiva and Dionysus. Rochester, Vt.: Inner Traditions International, 1992.
- ———. Hindu Polytheism. Rochester, Vt.: Inner Traditions International, 1991.
- Flood, Gavin. An Introduction to Hinduism. New Delhi: Cambridge University Press, 1998.
- Frawley, David. From the River of Heaven. Delhi: Motilal Banarsidass, 1992.
- Hawley, J. S. and D.M. Wulff, eds.. The Divine Consort. Boston: Beacon Press, 1982.
- Hopkins, E. Washburn. Epic Mythology. Delhi: Motilal Banarsidass, 1986.
- Jakimowicz-Shah, Marta. Metamorphosis of Indian Gods. Calcutta: Seagull Books, 1988.
- Kinsley, David. Hindu Goddesses. Delhi: Motilal Banarsidass, 1987.
- Klostermaier, Klaus K. Hinduism: A Short History. Oxford: Oneworld Publications, 2000.
- Knappert, Jan. An Encyclopedia of Myth and Legend: Indian Mythology. New Delhi: HarperCollins, 1992.
- Kosambi, Damodar Dharmanand. Myth and Reality. Mumbai: Popular Prakashan, Pvt. Ltd., 1994.
- Krishnan, Yuvraj. Ganesa: unraveling an enigma. Delhi: Motilal Banarsidass, 1999.
- Mani, Vettam. Puranic Encyclopaedia. Delhi: Motilal Banarsidass, 1996.
- Martin-Dubost, Paul. Ganesa: The Enchanter of the Three Worlds. Mumbai: Franco-Indian Research, 1997.
- Wilkins, W. J. Hindu Mythology. Delhi: Rupa, 1997.
- Zimmer, Heinrich. Myths and Symbols in Indian Art and Civilization. Delhi: Motilal Banarsidass, 1990.

Siddhi Vinayak of Mumbai, in whose garden
my mother sat long before my birth, when today's
temple tower was the simplest of shrines

– Devdutt Pattanaik

99 Thoughts on Ganesha

Devdutt Pattanaik

Illustrations by Devdutt Pattanaik
Photographs by Harpreet Chhachhiya

JAICO PUBLISHING HOUSE

Ahmedabad   Bangalore   Bhopal   Chennai
Delhi   Hyderabad   Kolkata   Lucknow   Mumbai

Published by Jaico Publishing House
A-2 Jash Chambers, 7-A Sir Phirozshah Mehta Road
Fort, Mumbai - 400 001
jaicopub@jaicobooks.com
www.jaicobooks.com

99 THOUGHTS ON GANESHA
ISBN 978-81-8495-152-3

First Jaico Impression: 2011

Design and typesetting by Special Effects, Mumbai

Printed by
Thomson Press (India) Limited
B-315, Okhla Phase-I, Industrial Area
New Delhi-110 020

In memory of my father whose name was Prafulla,
meaning 'gladness' and 'cheer'.

Contents

Author's Note

Ganesha is an organic god, transforming over space and time, geography and history. In Vedic times, all we had was his name. Later, the name came to be associated with malevolent spirits who had to be appeased. Then he came to acquire a form, one that connected him with feared forest beings, the Yakshas, and wild animals, the elephant and rats and serpents. Eventually he became a benevolent spirit, associated with vegetation, with betel leaves, areca nuts, turmeric, hibiscus and grass, whose name is invoked at the start of every ceremony. He was welcomed into the mainstream pantheon as the son of Shiva and Shakti and his fame spread as the patron deity of the medieval Maratha warlords during whose reign scriptures were written to his glory. During the freedom struggle, his worship became the rallying point of

communities. And in modern times, he has become the god who understands modernity and the youth and their yearning to break free from the shackles of tradition. Of all the gods in the Hindu pantheon, he alone allows his form to be re-shaped and re-imagined and recreated as devotees will it. Thus, he reminds us constantly that:

Within infinite myths lies the eternal truth
Who sees it all?
Varuna has but a thousand eyes
Indra, a hundred
You and I, only two

Part I

Creation

Devdutt Pattanaik

1

A Mythological Puzzle

The image of Ganesha, his rituals and his stories, are a kind of mythological puzzle created by our ancestors. Through him, they are trying to communicate a profound truth that changed their understanding of the world, and enabled them to live a richer fuller life. One can argue, why not simply give the solution; why go through the trouble of creating a puzzle? Ancient Hindus believed, wisdom must never be given. It has to be taken. And so, the answers are right there in front of us, in the form of Ganesha, if we are willing to decode it. If we do not want to do decode it, it's perfectly alright. The image of Ganesha will continue to enrich us, even without being intellectually analysed. The intellectual approach to Ganesha is called gyan yoga. The emotional approach to Ganesha is called bhakti yoga. And a mechanical, ritualistic, approach to Ganesha is called karma yoga. Different approaches for different people. All work.

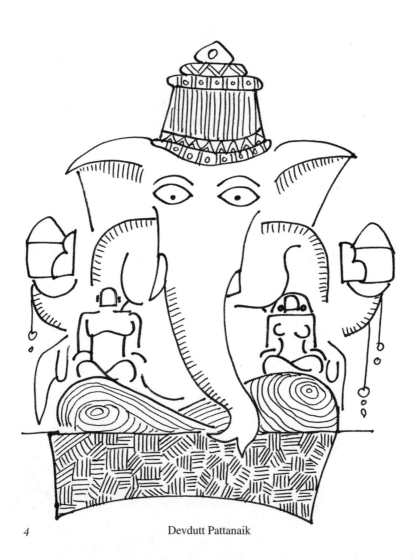

Devdutt Pattanaik

2

The Idea of Ganesha

L ife can be fun. Life can also be painful. Sometimes we wish to experience all the excitement of life. But then, we experience sorrow and frustration. We wish to withdraw from life. Our ancestors experienced this too and concluded that there are two ways to live life: as a hermit who steps back and contemplates on the nature of the world and as a householder who stays in the world and experiences all it has to offer fearlessly. Our ancestors visualized the hermit as Shiva, the male form of divinity, or God, and the householder as Shakti, the female form of divinity, i.e. the Goddess. Shiva does not want to be a father and to deal with the trials and tribulations of worldly life. Shakti wants to be a mother and to engage with all things worldly, but she knows she cannot do so with Shiva's support and participation. From this tension between hermit and householder, God and Goddess, is born Ganesha, his animal head representing material joys and his human body representing spiritual bliss. In Ganesha, God and Goddess attain balance, material pleasure and spiritual wisdom in harmony.

Devdutt Pattanaik

3

From Vinayaka to Ganesha

Though Shiva and Shakti are husband and wife, Shiva did not want to be a father. "I am God. I will never grow old or die. Why do I need children?" But Shakti wanted a child, one who will help all creatures realize God. She decided to create one on her own. She anointed herself with turmeric and oil. When the mixture had soaked her sweat and dried on her skin, she scraped it off and from the rubbings created a child, her son. She called him Vinayaka, a child created without (vina) the help of a man (nayaka), and ordered him to guard the gate of her cave and not let anyone in. Vinayaka, who had never seen Shiva, stopped everyone from entering his mother's cave, even Shiva. This infuriated Shiva so much he raised his trident and destroyed Vinayaka's head. When Shakti learnt of this, she was inconsolable in her grief. "I want my son back," she demanded. To pacify her, Shiva placed the head of an elephant on Vinayaka's headless body and resurrected him. Shiva declared him to be Ganesha or Ganapati, leader of his followers who are known as Ganas. This is how, without realizing it, Shiva became a father, much to Shakti's delight.

Devdutt Pattanaik

4

Shiva to Shankara

Shiva has two forms. Shiva is the form where his eyes are shut while Shankara is the form where his eyes are open. Shiva is indifferent to worldly matters. The shutting of Shiva's eyes causes all heat to be contained in his body, causing the world around him to become dark and cold and snow-clad. This is destruction. So the Goddess, Shakti, coaxes Shiva to open his eyes. The snow melts, the river flows, and life happens. In the Varaha Purana, it is said that when Shiva opened his eyes, he laughed and from that laughter was born Ganesha. But he looked just like Shiva. To distinguish father from son, Shakti gave her son an elephant's head, because an elephant's head represents material splendor. In other words, Ganesha marks the point when human consciousness stops being indifferent and willingly engages with the material world. In Shiva temples, the Shiva-linga is typically accompanied by images of Shakti as well as Ganesha to ensure that the deity does not forget that he is Shankara.

Devdutt Pattanaik

5

Kali to Gauri

Shakti has two forms, Kali, who is wild and ferocious and eternally thirsty for blood and Gauri, who is gentle and demure and domesticated and full of love. These are two aspects of nature, the life-taking and the life-giving. Kali takes the ferocious form when Shiva shuts his eyes. In this form, she dances on his body determined to make him open his eyes. When he opens his eyes, she becomes Gauri and sits on his lap and lovingly takes care of him. It is as Gauri that the Goddess becomes the mother of Ganesha. In the Brihaddharma Purana, it is said that Shiva took a cloth, tied it into knots and finally gave it the shape of an elephant-headed doll to pacify Kali. Kali placed this against her breasts and it was endowed with life. Thus was born Ganesha. His arrival transformed Kali into Gauri. Gauri is the earth. She is visualized as the milk-giving cow, making Ganesha her calf, whose arrival marks the arrival of milk, symbolizing harvest and prosperity. Significantly, worship of mother and son takes place twice a year, a reminder of India's two agricultural cycles, the rabi in spring and the kharif in autumn.

Devdutt Pattanaik

6

The Northern Direction

When Shiva promises to replace the head of Shakti's son, he instructs his followers, the Ganas, to go north and bring him the head of the first creature they encounter. Why north? The northern direction plays a key role in mythology. It is the direction marked by the Pole Star, the one star that does not move in the sky. This makes it the direction associated with stillness and stability and hence, wisdom. This makes south the direction of movement and instability and ignorance. Vastu-shastra describes the mythic structure of space. In it, north is ruled by Kubera, the pot-bellied treasurer of the gods while south is ruled by Yama, god of death. Since north is associated with prosperity, south becomes the direction of decay. Since south is the direction of death, north becomes the direction of immortality. Thus north becomes associated with all things auspicious: permanence, immortality, prosperity and wisdom. It is from here that Shiva seeks to replace the head of Shakti's child. In Tantra, Shiva is called Dakshina-murti, he who sits facing the south, and Shakti is called Dakshina-kali, she who walks from the south. Together they create Ganesha.

Devdutt Pattanaik

7

Gajantaka

There is a phrase in Hindi to describe liars, hypocrites and pretenders: "Elephants show one set of teeth (tusks), but chew with another set of teeth." In other words, what is spoken is not necessarily the truth. Elephants thus are a symbol of deception. This negative symbol transforms into a demon called Gaja-Asura. Shiva had no patience with Gajasura's wily nature so he flayed him alive, danced on his head and turned his blood-soaked skin into a robe. Shiva, the killer of the elephant-demon, Gajasura, is called Gajantaka. Having killed the demon, Shiva used this head to resurrect Shakti's son. The human body purged the demon of negative qualities and made the elephant head worthy of worship. The human body represents that one thing that animals do not possess – the imagination and intellect that enables human beings to overcome fear. It is fear that makes man a liar and a cheat; it is fear that makes man a hypocrite. If there were no fear, a man would have no need to pretend and say things he did not mean. Thus Ganesha's human body and animal head reminds us that we have the ability in ourselves to overpower the beast within us that is always afraid. In South Indian traditions, Ganesha himself overpowers an elephant-headed demon, Gajasura.

Devdutt Pattanaik

8

Airavata

When the Devas and the Asuras churned the ocean of milk, out came many treasures. One of them was a white-skinned elephant called Airavata. He became the vehicle of Indra, the sky-god, who shatters dark clouds with thunderbolts to release rain. Airavata is associated with rain and fertility. It is said that this was the elephant whose head was used to create Ganesha. This is why images of Ganesha in Bengal typically show the elephant head colored white. The Brihaddharma Purana, very explicitly states that when Nandi, the attendant of Shiva, was asked to fetch a head from the northern direction, he found Airavata on the foothills of the Himalayas and cut his head off. In India, where most people depend on agriculture for their livelihood, the monsoons play a key role in determining their economic fate. Not surprisingly the god who brings rain, Indra, and his elephant play a significant role in people's imagination. That Ganesha festivals are typically celebrated as the monsoon season is on a wane is an indicator of the close relationship between rains and elephants and Ganesha. As Ganesha grew in popularity and his worship was closely associated with wealth and fertility, it was but natural to associate him with Indra through Airavata.

Devdutt Pattanaik

9

The Second Mother

In Tibetan texts, there is the story of how Varahi, the boar-headed wife of Shiva, created a son. Out of jealousy, Shiva's other wife, Uma, cut the child's head. Shiva then restored the second head with that of an elephant's. In other Tibetan variants of the story, the wife who creates the child is Ganga, not Varahi, and Uma not only cuts the child's head in jealousy, she also resurrects it with an elephant's head later, out of compassion. In Padma Purana, the goddess Paravati creates a doll using the turmeric scrubbings of her body and immerses it in Ganga as a result of which it comes alive. The gods believe the child is Ganga's but Parvati claims it as her own. The Haracharitachintamani by Jayadhrata, dating back to 13th century, states that when Shakti was bathing, her elephant-headed attendant, whose name was Malini, extended her trunk and drank the bath water. That made her pregnant and she gave birth to a five-headed elephant boy, a wild being who needed to be tamed. The Goddess called out to Shiva who cut four of the elephant-boy's five heads but stopped short of killing him. The elephant-boy left with only one head bowed to Shiva and Shakti who accepted him as their son and declared him to be Ganesha, the first of the Ganas. All these stories explain why Ganesha is sometimes called dvi-mata, the one with two mothers.

Part II

Family

Devdutt Pattanaik

10

Durga

In Bengal, in autumn each year, goddess Durga returns to her father's house to spend ten days. It's a vacation for her, a break from her hermit husband, Shiva. She is visualized as coming home with her four children, two sons and two daughters. Her sons are Ganesha and Kartikeya. Her daughters are Lakshmi, the goddess of wealth, and Saraswati, the goddess of knowledge. Ganesha is visualized as an intellectual scribe while Kartikeya is visualized as a powerful warrior. The story goes that to look after her children, Durga has to fend for herself as Shiva does not contribute to the family. Her killing of the buffalo demon, Mahish-Asura, is a metaphor for the struggles she has to go through to defend her children and feed them. Durga is the earth that has to be domesticated in order, for man to get wealth or Lakshmi. To protect this domesticated earth, one needs Kartikeya. The knowledge required to domesticate earth comes from Saraswati. And Ganesha maintains the records of the wealth generated. While Lakshmi and Kartikeya take care of material needs, Saraswati and Ganesha take care of intellectual and spiritual needs. The earth satisfies all our needs. But sometimes man forgets that he is the beneficiary of the earth's goodness. He deludes himself that he is the master of the earth. That is when Durga rises with her trident and impales the demon who assumes he can control her, thus justifying her name Durga which means the 'invincible one'.

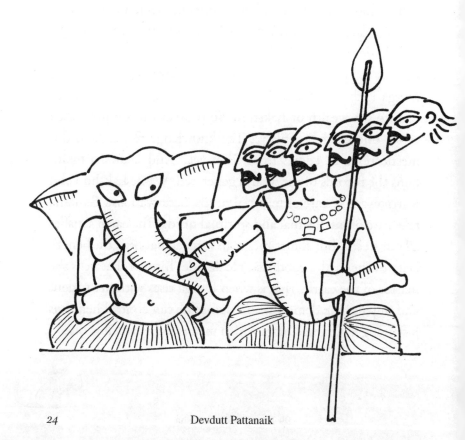

Devdutt Pattanaik

11

Kartikeya

Ganesha has a brother called Kartikeya. Like Ganesha, Kartikeya is created differently outside his mother's body. The Devas did not want Kartikeya to be conceived inside Shakti so they interrupted the lovemaking of Shiva and Shakti and caused Shiva to spill his semen outside. This semen was then incubated by the fire-god, Agni, by the wind-god, Vayu, by the river-goddess, Ganga, by the forest of reeds, Saravan, and by the six stars that form the Pleiades constellation, the Krittikas. Finally, he was given his final form, one with six human heads, and granted a weapon, a spear, by Shakti, completing his creation. Thus while Ganesha's creation is started by Shakti (creating a doll out of the remains of the dried turmeric on her body) and concluded by Shiva (replacing the human head with an animal head), Kartikeya's creation is started by Shiva (spilling semen) and concluded by Shakti (granting him a weapon). The two brothers represent two ends of the spectrum. They complement each other. Ganesha is obese while Kartikeya is muscular. Ganesha is commonly visualized as a scribe who helped Vyasa write the epic, Mahabharata, while Kartikeya is visualized as a warlord who helped Indra, king of the gods, defeat the demon, Taraka. Ganesha ensures prosperity while Kartikeya provides protection. Together they ensure happiness in the world created by the union of their parents, Shiva and Shakti.

Devdutt Pattanaik

12

Marriage

Is Ganesha married or single? There is no consensus on this. For some, especially in the bhakti or devotional traditions, he is a boy-god, a child, while for others, especially in the tantra or occult traditions, he is a fully grown matured deity. In South India, typically, he is visualized as the learned boy who refuses to marry until he meets a girl who is as wonderful as his mother. No woman is, as a result, good enough for him. He remains single while his brother, Kartikeya is married with two wives, Valli and Sena. In North India typically, Ganesha is visualized with two wives, Riddhi and Siddhi (or Buddhi). In Tantrik texts, he is often shown with a female companion identified as his Shakti. Marriage is a metaphor in Hindu mythology for worldliness. A bachelor Ganesha indicates the hermit way of living suitable for students and for retired people where the focus is on celibacy and spiritual pursuits. A married Ganesha indicates the householder's way of living where there is celebration of sensuality and material desires. Thus in the two forms, Ganesha addresses all needs of man in every stage of life, as a student, a householder, and a retired person.

Devdutt Pattanaik

13

Riddhi, Siddhi, Buddhi

Brahma, the creator, is often called Prajapati, which means father of all living creatures. From his mind, Brahma created two daughters, Siddhi and Riddhi. These daughters were given to Ganesha in marriage. Sometimes, the daughters are identified as Riddhi and Buddhi. Riddhi represents material growth and prosperity. Buddhi and Siddhi represent intellectual growth and wisdom. Not much is known about these two goddesses and there are no special rituals for them. In some temples, they appear on either side of Ganesha, fanning him with peacock feathers or a yak-tail fly whisk known as chamar. They are almost like maids with no personality of their own. The two wives of Ganesha embody the two things that enter our lives when we worship Ganesha – prosperity and wisdom. They represent two key desires of man, wealth and wisdom, visualized in female forms.

Devdutt Pattanaik

14

Lakshmi

Lakshmi, the goddess of wealth, seated on a lotus, holding a pot overflowing with grain and gold is closely associated with Ganesha. In her images, she is always flanked by white elephants with upraised trunks spraying her with milk and water. The spraying of water by elephants alludes to rain and prosperity. In Bengal, images of Lakshmi are placed next to images of Ganesha when the new Halkatha or account books are opened during the festival marking the spring equinox, Poila Boishak. This festival was the time when the Mughal rulers finally completed the taxation process and it was time to celebrate. Thus it was a time of bounty and excitement. Bounty, to celebrate the harvest of the previous year and excitement, in anticipation of what is going to happen in the following year. Lakshmi's image then represents the bounty that has come from the previous year while Ganesha's image represents the hope for the following year which should ideally be free from all obstacles. The relationship between Lakshmi and Ganesha is unclear. In Bengal tradition, they are siblings, children of Durga. In other traditions, they are mother and son, Lakshmi being just another form of Gauri. Then there are traditions where Lakshmi is the wife of Ganesha; she is a more elaborated form of Riddhi, the goddess associated with material accomplishments. Lakshmi with Ganesha is an essential part of worship in business establishments.

Devdutt Pattanaik

15

Saraswati

Saraswati, goddess of knowledge and learning, dressed in serene white, holding a lute or veena in her hand, and a book and a string of memory beads, is closely associated with Ganesha. This is typically seen in manuscripts that originate in Maharashtra. The goddess is visualized riding a gander, or the hamsa. This bird is believed to have the unique ability to separate milk from water, making it the symbol of intellectual discrimination, having the ability to distinguish truth from falsehood. The goddess is also visualized riding a heron, who stands on one foot in water and waits patiently for a fish, making the heron a symbol of concentration. Education is impossible without Ganesha who removes obstacles in the path of learning and enlightenment. In Bengal, Saraswati and Ganesha are siblings, children of Durga. Some say that Ganesha is Saraswati's child, for when one is learned one knows how to overpower obstacles. Some identify Saraswati as an elaborated form of Buddhi or Siddhi, the consort of Ganesha. Cynics say that the two are also patrons of thieves – for the heron of Saraswati is the symbol of a crafty sage who stands on one foot pretending to be in meditation but actually is crying to beguile a fish and catch it for food, while the elephant head of Ganesha is the symbol of hypocrisy, who shows the tusk but eats with the teeth. Even thieves need knowledge, even thieves need luck, which is essentially freedom from obstacles.

Devdutt Pattanaik

16

Lakshmi and Saraswati

Lakshmi, is the goddess of wealth. When she enters the house, there is prosperity. Saraswati, is the goddess of wisdom. When she enters the house, there is peace. But the two of them do not stay in the same house which is why peace and prosperity rarely co-exist. Lakshmi loves to visit the places where Saraswati resides. But her arrival marks the end of wisdom and peace. With wealth comes quarrels, bickering over money-matters, annoying Saraswati who runs away. The two goddesses are described as quarrelling sisters. The only god who can bring them together is Ganesha. That is why the images of Lakshmi and Saraswati with Ganesha in the middle are very popular. Lakshmi is dressed in red and is covered with jewels. Saraswati wears a simple white sari and does not care for jewels. Lakshmi is associated with lotus flowers and pots and baskets overflowing with grain and gold. Saraswati is associated with books and memory beads and musical instruments. Lakshmi brings material pleasure in her wake; Saraswati brings intellectual bliss. To have both together, one has to pray to Ganesha.

Devdutt Pattanaik

17

Kola Bau

No one in the world wants to marry Ganesha because of his elephant-head, no woman is ready to be his bride. To make him happy, his mother Durga takes the banana plant, wraps a sari around it and gives it in marriage to Ganesha who is overjoyed. A banana plant wrapped in a sari is therefore kept next to Ganesha during Durga Puja. She is known as 'Kola Bau.' Kola Bau, which loosely translated means 'matriarch of the household', is identified by some devotees as the wife of Ganesha, but by others as simply another form of Durga, hence Ganesha's mother. During Dassera, Durga is worshipped as a collective of nine medicinal and edible plants. Eight of these herbs are tied around the stem of the Banana plant and then draped in a red white sari on the seventh day of the nine-night festival of Navaratri. This is the eve of the main festival. Thus Durga is visualized as Shakambari, the goddess of vegetation. This is Kola Bau, the vegetable goddess, who sustains the household. Her association with Ganesha, the god who brings good luck into the household, is understandable.

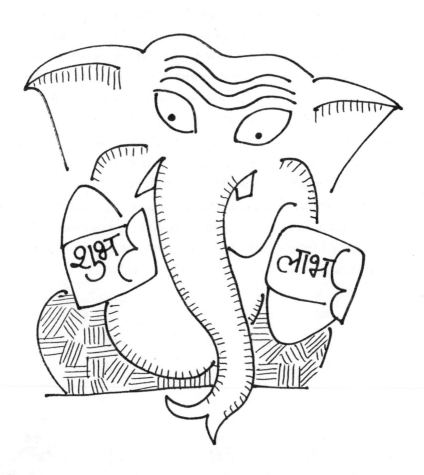

Devdutt Pattanaik

18

Shubha and Labha

If Riddhi and Buddhi are the wives of Ganesha, his children are Kshema or prosperity and Labha or profit. In other parts of India, the children of Ganesha are identified as Shubha and Labha meaning auspiciousness and profit. Lakshmi or Riddhi brings forth prosperity and profit, while Saraswati or Buddhi brings forth Shubha or auspiciousness. Like his wives, not much is known about the children of Ganesha, suggesting that more than being mythological characters they are metaphysical ideas. When Ganesha enters our life, he is accompanied by wealth and fortune on one hand as well as wisdom and auspiciousness on the other. The names of Ganesha's children are often written on the walls of houses, usually at the entrance on either side of Ganesha's image placed atop the doorway. He keeps away bad luck and misfortune and brings in good luck and fortune. Unlike Labha which everyone understands, the word Shubh is often difficult to explain to non-Indians as it indicates good luck, sacredness, beauty and empowerment, all at the same time.

Devdutt Pattanaik

19

Santoshi

In 1975 a low-budget film called "Jai Santoshi-maa", became a Bollywood blockbuster. This film introduced Indians to a new goddess, until then a folk goddess, called Santoshi, who became a part of mainstream Hinduism. As goddess of contentment, she was worshipped by housewives who sought reprieve from domestic problems. Her worship takes place on Fridays, a day closely associated with Lakshmi, and involves eating only Bengal gram and jaggery, and avoiding sour food. If Santoshi is worshipped over sixteen Fridays she grants the wishes of her devotees. The film identified Santoshi as the daughter of Ganesha, indicating that when Ganesha enters the lives of devotees along with Riddhi and Siddhi, he is followed not just by his sons, profit and auspiciousness, but also by his daughter, satisfaction.

Devdutt Pattanaik

20

Vinayaki

Vinayaki is the female Ganesha. The demon, Andhaka, wanted the goddess Parvati to be his wife. He tried to grab her by force so she called out to her husband, Shiva who immediately raised his trident and impaled the Asura. But the Asura had a magic power; every drop of his blood that touched the ground turned into another Andhaka. The only way to kill him was to ensure that not a single drop of his blood touched the ground, while he was impaled on Shiva's trident. Parvati therefore called out to all the Shaktis. Both Shiva and Parvati knew that every divine being is a mixture of male and female forms, the male form representing spiritual reality and the female form representing material reality. So Parvati requested the female energy, also known as Shakti, to be released from every divine being, so as to drink the blood of Andhaka before it touched the ground. Soon the battlefield was filled with the shaktis of every god imaginable. Indra's shakti emerged as Indrani, Vishnu's shakti emerged as Vaishnavi and Brahma's shakti emerged as Brahmini. Matsya Purana and Vishnu-dharmottara Purana list even Ganesha's shakti in the list of female warrior goddesses. Her name was Vinayaki, she was also known as Ganeshvari. This form of Ganesha is adored in the Vana-Durga-Upanishad.

Part III

Representations

Devdutt Pattanaik

21

4 Forms

A peculiar feature of all Vishnu stories is that he descends from his paradise known as Vaikuntha and descends on earth to solve various worldly problems. This descent or avatarana results in various Vishnu incarnations or avatars. Thus Ram, the model king, is an avatar of Vishnu as is Krishna, the winsome cowherd. The idea of Vishnu's avatars appealed to all Hindus so much that worshippers of other deities also narrated tales describing the avatars of their gods and goddesses. Thus Shaivas told tales of Shiva's avatars and Shaktas told tales of Shakti's avatars. Ganapatyas did the same. Ganesh Purana refers to four avatars of Ganesha, each taken in each of the four yugas.

- In the Krita Yuga, riding a lion, he killed the demon brothers Narantaka and Devantaka.

- In the Treta Yuga, riding a peacock, he killed the demon Sindhu.

- In the Dvapara yuga, riding a rat, he killed the demon Sindura.

- In the Kali Yuga, which is currently on, he will ride a horse, just like Vishnu's Kalki avatar, and assuming the form of Dhumraketu, he will kill the demon.

Devdutt Pattanaik

22

8 Avatars

In the Mudgala Purana, Ganesha takes eight forms to destroy eight demons, each demon representing a disruptive emotional state.

- Vakratunda (god with curved trunk) rides a lion to kill Matsara, the demon of jealousy

- Ekadanta (god with one tusk) rides a rat to kill Mada, the demon of vanity

- Mahodara (god with great belly) rides a rat to kill Moha, the demon of attachment

- Gajanana (god with elephant head) rides a rat to kill Lobha, the demon of greed

- Lambodara (god with pot belly) rides a rat to kill Krodha, the demon of rage

- Vikata (god with deformed body) rides a peacock to overpower Kama, the lord of lust

- Vighnaraja (master of obstacles) rides a serpent to kill Mama, the demon of self indulgence

- Dhumravarna (smoke-colored god) rides a rat to kill Ahamkara, the demon of arrogance

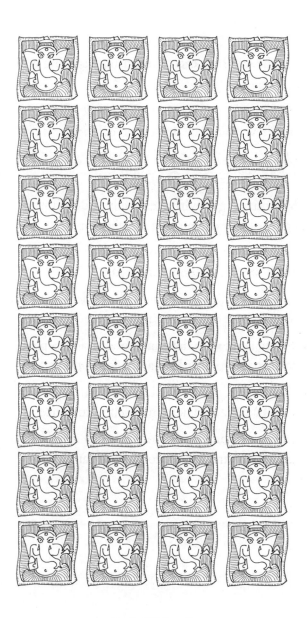

Devdutt Pattanaik

23

32 Images

In the 19th century, the king of Mysore of the Wodayar dynasty, ordered the court scholars to make a comprehensive list of all images of the gods. This resulted in a compilation known as Sri-tattva-nidhi written in Kannada where there are lists of various forms of the most worshipped Hindu gods. In this compilation, one finds 32 various forms of Ganesha, perhaps images that the artisans found being worshipped in the various temples and households in the kingdom. These various forms of Ganesha are:

1. **Bala Ganapathi:** The child-like Ganesha 2. **Taruna Ganapathi:** The youthful Ganesha 3. **Bhakti Ganapathi:** The devotion-worthy Ganesha 4. **Veera Ganapathi:** The valiant Ganesha 5. **Shakti Ganapathi:** Ganesha with his strength seated in female form on his left lap 6. **Dvija Ganapathi:** Twice born or student Ganesha 7. **Siddhi Ganapathi:** The accomplished Ganesha 8. **Ucchishta Ganapathi:** The Ganesha who accepts offerings 9. **Vighna Ganapathi:** The obstacle-removing Ganesha 10. **Kshipra Ganapathi:** The quick acting Ganesha 11. **Heramba Ganapathi:** The fierce Ganesha 12. **Lakshmi Ganapathi:** Ganesha with the goddess of wealth 13. **Maha Ganapathi** The great Ganesha 14. **Vijaya Ganapathi:** The triumphant Ganesha 15. **Nritta Ganapathi:** The dancing Ganesha 16. **Urdhva Ganapathi:** The restrained Ganesha 17. **Ekakshara Ganapathi:** The single syllable Ganesha 18. **Vara Ganapathi:** The boon bestowing Ganesha 19. **Tryakshara Ganapathi:** The three syllable Ganesha 20. **Kshipraprasaada Ganapathi:** The hastily benevolent Ganesha 21. **Haridra Ganapathi:** The golden Ganesha 22. **Ekadhanta Ganapathi:** The one-toothed Ganesha 23. **Srishti Ganapathi:** The cosmic Ganesha 24. **Udanda Ganapathi:** The disciplinarian Ganesha 25. **Ranamochana Ganapathi:** The debt-redeeming Ganesha 26. **Dundi Ganapathi:** The desired Ganesha 27. **Dvimukha Ganapathi:** Two-headed Ganesha 28. **Trimukha Ganapathi:** Three-headed Ganesha 29. **Simha Ganapathi:** Lion-riding Ganesha 30. **Yoga Ganapathi:** Ganesha as yogi 31. **Durga Ganapathi:** Invincible Ganesha 32. **Sankatahara Ganapathi:** The problem-solving Ganesha.

Devdutt Pattanaik

24

Collective

Ganesha images are often seen along with the Nava-Graha collective or the Sapta-Matrika collective. The Nava-Grahas are nine male deities who represent the nine celestial bodies that play a key role in astrology. Sapta-Matrikas are seven female deities who are associated with diseases that affect children; they cause fevers, pox infections, seizures and miscarriages. Both these sets of deities can be malevolent. The alignment of the nine planets can bring bad luck into one's life and the gaze of the seven goddesses can wreak havoc in a household. As Ganesha grew in popularity and moved from being a folk deity to a mainstream deity, he was called upon to control or mitigate the negative effects caused by the Nava-Grahas and the Sapta-Matrikas. Thus he became the god who removes obstacles.

Part IV

Stories

Devdutt Pattanaik

25

Lord of Obstacles

The gods once churned the ocean of milk for the nectar of immortality known as amrita. However, they forgot to propitiate Ganesha before this undertaking. To teach them a lesson, Ganesha caused the serpent-king Vasuki who was being used as the churning rope to vomit out venom. As the gods choked on the poison, they invoked Ganesha and begged him to remove this obstacle to their success. Pleased with their worship, Ganesha requested his father Shiva to drink and digest the poison, thus clearing the air and enabling the gods to continue churning until the pot of elixir emerged from the ocean. Since then, everyone worships Ganesha. Without propitiating him, they say, Krishna could not have married Rukmini, Ram could not have killed Ravan, Kartikeya could not have killed Taraka, Shiva could not have killed the Tripura demons, Durga could not have killed Mahisha, and Rishis could not have attained wisdom. Ganesha's name is chanted before any activity is started. Those who forget to do so, do so at their own peril.

Devdutt Pattanaik

26

Parashuram

Whenever there are problems on earth, Vishnu descends from his heaven, Vaikuntha, and takes an appropriate animal or human form to set things right. The sixth such form of Vishnu is that of Parashurama who killed many unrighteous kings with his axe. According to Brahmanda Purana and Brahmavaivarta Purana, towards the end of his stay on earth, Parashurama decided to give his blood soaked axe to Shiva. So he made his way to Mount Kailas, the abode of Shiva. Ganesha stood guard at the foothills of Mount Kailas and would not let Parashurama in until he introduced himself. But Parashurama was in too much of a hurry to do so. So he pushed Ganesha away. Ganesha refused to budge. Irritated, Parashurama swung his axe and struck one of Ganesha's tusks. That is how it is said to have broken. Ganesh's mother, Parvati, was so angry when she saw this that she transformed into Durga, the fierce warrior goddess, and challenged Parashurama to a duel. Parashurama realized he had acted harshly and apologized to the goddess. She calmed down, but on condition that Parashurama give up his axe. Parashurama did as instructed and gave the axe to Ganesha in whose hand it can still be seen in images today. With the axe gone, Parashurama was no longer the angry warrior-priest. He became a sage and meditated on the foothills of Mount Kailas.

Devdutt Pattanaik

27

The Moon

One day the moon laughed when he saw Ganesha riding on a rat because he found the idea of a elephant-headed fat god riding a tiny rodent rather amusing. Ganesha did not appreciate the moon god's laughter and so declared that anyone who looked at the moon on the fourth day of the waxing moon in the month of Bhadrapada, which is sacred to Ganesha, will suffer bad luck. This is why no one looks at the moon on Ganesha Chaturthi.

Devdutt Pattanaik

28

Syamantaka

Vishnu lives in his heaven, Vaikuntha. But from time to time, he descends on earth as an avatar, either a human or an animal, to restore order. The eighth such form of Vishnu is that of Krishna who lived in the city of Mathura. A Yadava nobleman from Mathura called Satrajit received from the sun-god a jewel called Syamantaka. Krishna felt a jewel such as this should not be owned by any individual. Satrajit disagreed and gave it to his brother Prasenajit who wore it when he went out on a hunt. Prasenajit was discovered dead in the forest, the jewel missing from around his neck. Everyone assumed the murderer and thief was Krishna, until Krishna tracked the real killer, a lion, and the real thief, a bear. Krishna wondered why everyone was eager to believe he was a thief. In response, the sages said that years ago, when he was in Vrindavan, he had upset Ganesha by looking at the moon on Ganesha Chaturthi. Though Krishna, on his mother's instruction had not looked at the sky, he had glanced at the moon reflected on a bowl of milk he was carrying home. As a result the curse of Ganesha fell upon him and that is why people were eager to believe that Krishna had stolen the Syamantaka jewel. In the Padma Purana, Ganesha's tusk is broken not by Parashurama but by Krishna's elder brother, Balarama, using his pestle, perhaps in retaliation to this event.

Devdutt Pattanaik

29

Race

One day, Narada came to Mount Kailasa with a mango and he offered to give it to one of Shiva's sons, the one who was faster, the one who could go around the world three times before the other. Determined to win the race and get the mango, Kartikeya leapt on a peacock and flew around the mountains and the oceans and the continents, once, twice and thrice. But Ganesha did not budge. He sat next to his parents, Shiva and Shakti, playing with his rat. Just when Kartikeya was about to complete the third round, Ganesha ran around his parents three times and declared he had won! "How come?" asked Kartikeya and Ganesha replied, "You went around the world while I went around my world. You went around the objective world while I went around my subjective world. You went around the physical world around us while I went around an emotional world within me. What matters more?" For Kartikeya the measurable rational logical world mattered more than the unmeasurable emotional world that mattered to Ganesha. These are two aspects of life. Narada gave the mango to Ganesha. Kartikeya did not agree with this decision, and moved south.

Devdutt Pattanaik

30

Valli's Marriage

Kartikeya, the brother of Ganesha, is also known as Muruga, especially in Tamil Nadu. He lives in the mountains of Tamil Nadu and in one of the valleys, in the middle of a millet field, he saw a beautiful tribal girl called Valli. He fell in love with her but no matter how hard he tried she refused to respond to his attentions. So finally he prayed to his brother, Ganesha, who took the form of a wild elephant and stormed into the millet field frightening Valli who ran into the arms of the handsome-god Muruga. Muruga immediately offered protection to Valli and drove the elephant away much to her delight. Thus with the help of his brother, Muruga was finally able to get the girl of his dreams.

Devdutt Pattanaik

31

Vyasa's Scribe

The sage Vyasa had witnessed the events of the epic known as the Mahabharata. But all his thoughts were scrambled and tied in knots. So he invoked Ganesha to help him untangle these knots, organize his thoughts and document them. Ganesha therefore became Vyasa's scribe, writing down without stopping for a moment the great epic, which contains all knowledge. This is supposed to have taken place on the day known as Akshaya Tritiya, the third day of the waxing moon in the month of Vaishaka.

Devdutt Pattanaik

32

Kaveri

There was once a great drought in South India. The people there invoked Ganesha and begged him to save them. Ganesha requested his father Shiva to make his disciple Agastya go south with a pitcher of Ganga water. After crossing the Vindhya range, Agastya placed the pitcher on a mountain and began to meditate. Taking the form of a crow, Ganesha tipped this pitcher and caused the water of Ganga to flow across South India in the form of the river Kaveri. With the water came prosperity and joy.

Devdutt Pattanaik

33

Ravan

Shiva once allowed the demon-king Ravana to carry him to the city of Lanka in the form of a linga on condition that the sacred stone should never be placed on the ground before reaching its destination. The gods feared that no sooner did the linga reach Lanka than Ravana would become invincible. So they sought the help of Ganesha who made Ravana experience an uncontrollable urge to answer a call of nature. Desperate to relieve himself, Ravana requested a cowherd to hold the linga until he returned. The cowherd was none other than Ganesha himself. As soon as he was given the linga, he placed it on the ground where it took permanent root and became renowned as Mahabaleshwara. This story comes from the 15th century text, Gurucharitra, by Saraswati Gangadhara.

Devdutt Pattanaik

34

Vibhishan

While Ravan was a devotee of Shiva, his brother Vibhishana was a devotee of Vishnu. While attending the coronation of Ram, he was offered a gift. Vibhishana asked for the sacred image of Vishnu that was worshipped by Ram's family. This was the image of Ranganatha, Vishnu reclining on the coils of the serpent with many hoods, Adi Sesha. Ram gave it to him but warned him never to place it on the ground until he reached his destination. As Vibhishana made his way to Lanka, the gods begged Ganesha to intervene and stop the image from going to the land of Rakshasas. On the banks of the Kaveri, Ganesha caused Vibhishana's bladder to become full. Ganesha then took the form of a cowherd, offered to hold the image of Ranganatha while Vibhishana answered the call of nature. While Vibhishana was away, Ganesha placed the image on the ground, angering Vibhishana who chased the cowherd up a hill and struck him on his head on catching up with him at the summit. As a result, Ganesha got rooted to the spot. He became the famous Ganesha of the rock-fort temple of Trichy. Ranganatha became the lord of Srirangam. This image of Vishnu faces the south, not the auspicious east, so that every morning he can see his devotee, Vibhishana, brother of Ravana.

Devdutt Pattanaik

35

Kuber

Kuber is the treasurer of the gods, and a devotee of Shiva. Shiva is an ascetic with no wealth. Kuber saw that Shiva's son Ganesha was fat and had a huge appetite for sweets. He felt sorry for Shiva and wondered how he could feed this glutton of a son. He felt sorry for Ganesha too and concluded that he must be going hungry to bed most of the time. So Kuber offered to feed Ganesha one day. "How much will you feed me?" asked Ganesha. "As much as you wish," said Kuber. So Ganesha went to Kuber's kitchen and sat down to eat. He ate whatever was served before him, until the kitchen was empty. Kuber then ordered his servants to go out and buy more food. To Kuber's surprise, Ganesha ate all that was bought. So more food was fetched from distant granaries and Ganesha ate all that food too. As time passed, Kuber saw all his wealth depleting. Ganesha kept eating and there was no end in sight. Kuber then realized that he was being taught a lesson by Shiva and Ganesha. He thought that with his wealth he could feed God. God is infinite while his wealth was finite. He had been arrogant about his wealth and had not understood the true nature of divinity. He fell at Ganesha's feet and apologized.

Devdutt Pattanaik

36

Ganga to Godavari

Shiva's consort, Gauri, resented that the river-goddess, Ganga, sat on Shiva's head. So Gauri instructed Ganesha to find a way to get rid of the river-goddess. Ganesha took the form of a cowherd and went south to the hermitage of a sage called Gautama, a sage so powerful that in times of drought only he had the ability to feed and sustain the gods. Accompanying Ganesha was Jaya, Gauri's companion. Jaya took the form of a cow and began eating the plants in Gautama's garden. To stop the cow, Gautama struck her with a blade of grass. Jaya immediately fell down and pretended to be dead. Gautama was filled with fear for killing a cow is the worst of sins. Ganesha advised Gautama to bathe in the Ganga. "But I cannot leave my hermitage," said the sage. "In that case, do request the gods whom you fed during the drought to make Ganga come to you." Gautama followed this advice. The gods approached Shiva on Gautama's behalf and begged him to release Ganga from his hair so that she could travel south and flow beside Gautama's hermitage. Shiva agreed. Since then Ganga flows in the south as the river Godavari.

Devdutt Pattanaik

37

Divodasa

Shiva wanted to stay in Kashi but its king Divodasa would not let him in. To remove this obstacle, Shiva invoked Ganesha who took the form of Dhundi, the deluder, and caused Divodasa to turn away from the path of righteous conduct. As a result, the residents of Kashi revolted against their king and drove him out. With Divodasa gone, Shiva could enter his favorite city. Shiva ensured that the people of Kashi worshipped not only him but also Ganesha who established himself in the centre of the city in the form of Dhundiraja.

Devdutt Pattanaik

38

Paradise

This is how Ganesha-loka is described in the Ganesha Purana: "In the Sva-anand-bhavan, or paradise of Ganesha, he sits with Siddhi and Buddhi by his side, on a vast throne placed on a thousand petalled lotus, that rises in the middle of Ikshu-sagara, the ocean of sugarcane juice. His eyes are the sun and the moon and the earth is in his stomach. Devotion takes one to this place. One has to cross many worlds filled with demons and goblins and gnomes. Then one has to cross great darkness before reaching Sva-anand-bhavan. There, in the presence of Ganesha, one can bathe in sugarcane juice and drink sugarcane juice, and realize such bliss that there will be no desire for rebirth."

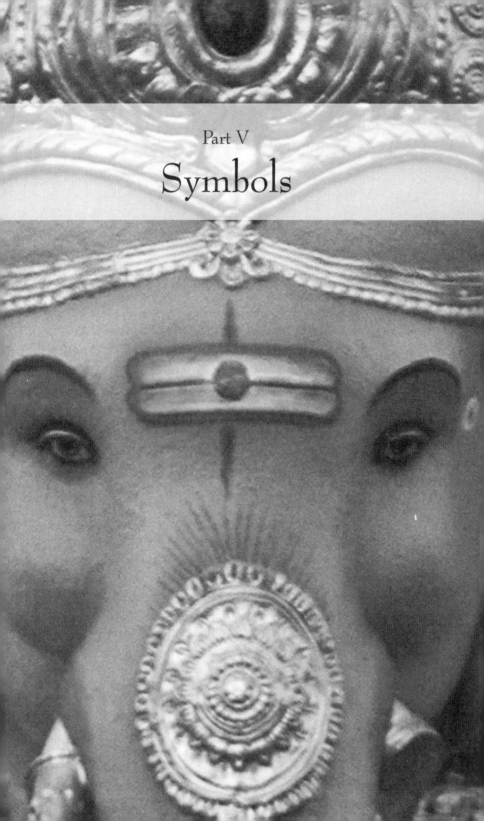

Part V
Symbols

Devdutt Pattanaik

39

Elephant Head

Ganesha's elephant head is a potent symbol of material reality – it represents prosperity and power. Only a rich fertile ecosystem can sustain an elephant. That an elephant exists on a land indicates that the land is well watered and has enough vegetation to sustain this mighty beast. In ancient times, only kings could afford to keep elephants as pets. An elephant is thus the ultimate symbol of wealth and power, a suitable companion of Lakshmi, goddess of wealth. The elephant also is the largest animal in the forest with no natural enemy and unstoppable because of its sheer strength and size. This makes it a creature of fortune, specially favoured by the gods. The elephant is also a symbol of sexual power. When the bull elephant is aroused, a state known as 'musht', it becomes violent and uncontrollable. From its temples a fluid oozes out 'mada' or ichor which is the symbol of obsessive passion. In Sanskrit, the phrase 'walking like a sexually aroused cow-elephant' is used to describe beautiful sensuous women. Elephants thus represent the material world in its full splendour, powerful and passionate. That an elephant head is placed on a human body suggests that in Ganesha, Shiva and Shakti want the potent raw animal power of the beast to be harnessed by the intellectual power of humans.

Devdutt Pattanaik

40

Human Body

The fundamental difference between humans and animals is the human brain, housed in the human head. This brain has one power that animals do not possess – humans can imagine. Humans can imagine a world that is better than the world one currently lives in, where the rat no longer fears the snake and the snake no longer fears the peacock. In other words, a world where there is no predator or prey. Humans can also imagine a world that is worse than the one we live in, a world of drought and hunger and suffering. And that generates the feeling of gratefulness for whatever we have. The human brain not only imagines but comes up with creative solutions such as tools to domesticate nature and rules to domesticate the mind. But most human beings do not use the human brain to outgrow their animal instincts. Instead they use their imagination to amplify their fears and in a state of insecurity become more territorial and dominating than animals. By creating a child who is half human and half animal, Shiva and Shakti draw the attention of devotees to their animal side and their human side. Only when humans realize that they have been blessed with the intellectual wherewithal to outgrow animal needs and fears, will they truly evolve and discover their potential.

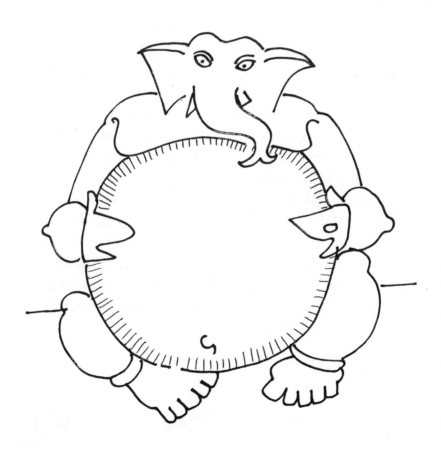

Devdutt Pattanaik

41

Pot Belly Lambodara

Ganesha is described as one with a vast framework and a pot-belly. In Ayurveda, the ancient Vedic way of health, this body would be described as Kapha – one that is water-based or fluid. Kapha is responsible for lubricating the body. Being fluid, Kapha can slip in anywhere and accommodate itself in any space. This is in keeping with Ganesha's role as a liminal being occupying the threshold between material and spiritual reality. In most ancient cultures, unlike modern ones, a fat body was worshipped and seen as the symbol of good luck. For it indicated abundance and relaxation and joy. For anyone who possessed such a body clearly had a lot of wealth and did not have to work too hard to earn that wealth and did not have stress gnawing at his health. In material terms, Ganesha's body indicates affluence as well as repose, success with least effort.

42

Curved Trunk

Ganesha is called Vakratunda, one whose trunk is turned to one side, either left or right. The left side is associated with the beating heart and traditionally the side associated with the material world. This makes the silent right side the side of spiritual reality. Shiva, the hermit, who rejects all things material therefore stands on only one foot, the right foot. Vishnu, the worldly god, by contrast, in the form of Krishna stands on both feet, takes the right foot across the left foot and places it on the ground, indicating that material life needs to experienced within the context of spiritual reality. The same ideas are indicated through the image of Ganesha. When Ganesha's trunk points to his left, and is closer to his heart, it indicates the more worldly form of Ganesha while when his trunk points to the right, away from the heart, it indicates a more ascetic form of Ganesha. The former worldly form is usually kept inside the house while the latter ascetic form is usually kept outside the house, in temples.

Devdutt Pattanaik

43

Red Color

Ganesha is often visualized in red color. Red color is significant in Hinduism because it represents material reality as opposed to white color which represents spiritual reality. The goddess, in her virginal form, wears a red sari while in her maternal form wears a green sari, like the red earth before rains and the green earth after rains. Ganesha's red color thus closely associates him with Shakti. It indicates he is fiery and energetic. He is called Mangal murti or the embodiment of auspiciousness. Mangal means auspicious. It also means the planet Mars, or Mangal Graha, the planet of aggressiveness with which even his brother, Kartikeya, warlord of the gods, is associated. This is also the reason that Tuesday, or the weekday associated with Mars, is also considered auspicious for Ganesha rituals.

Devdutt Pattanaik

44

Axe and Noose

In one hand, Ganesha holds the Parashu and in the other he holds the Pasha. Parashu or axe is the symbol of analysis, the act of breaking things down into tiny constituent elements and studying each element for its individual distinguishing characteristics. Pasha or noose is the symbol of synthesis, the act of binding together things after they have been broken down. Parashu involves seeking the parts of the whole; the trees of the forest. Pasha involves seeing the whole made of parts; the forest made of the trees. Parashu is about disintegrating and Pasha is about reintegrating. Together, they represent the two abilities of the human mind to understand material reality and by doing so realizing spiritual reality.

Devdutt Pattanaik

45

Goad

Ganesha is often shown holding an elephant goad or Ankusha. The elephant goad is a powerful instrument with two parts. The first part is the sharp tip with which the elephant keeper or Mahout goads the elephant to move forward. The second part is the hook with which the Mahout restrains the elephant. Thus it is a symbol of both encouragement and restraint. The human Mahout uses the goad to tame the wild elephant and put it to good domestic use. The elephant goad is a reminder that within all of us is animal power waiting to be encouraged and which, from time to time, needs to be restrained. In balance lies happiness.

Devdutt Pattanaik

46

Sugarcane

Sugarcane is associated with Kama, god of love and desire. It is the shaft of the love-god's bow. Ganesha is often shown holding a sugarcane in his hands indicating his association with all things material and sensual. Sugarcane contains sweet juicy fluid that is considered symbolic of rasa, or the juice of life, that one has to suck out as one experiences the world. Ganesha's paradise is said to be located in the middle of the ocean of sugarcane juice. Besides the sugarcane, Ganesha is visualized with other fruits associated with wealth and prosperity, such as the banana (kadali), coconut (naral), the jackfruit (phanas), the rose apple (jamun) and the wood apple (bilva).

Devdutt Pattanaik

47

Single Tusk

Ganesha is Ekadanta, he who has a single tusk. Usually the left tusk is broken, but this is not consistent across images. An elephant with two giant tusks represents aggression and violence. To tame the elephant, make it less wild and more domestic, one of Ganesha's tusks is broken. Skanda Purana states that he broke it himself. Bhavishya Purana says it was broken by his brother, Kartikeya. Brahmanda Purana says it was broken during a duel with Parashurama while Padma Purana states it was broken by Balarama in a duel. The broken tusk serves many purposes. It serves as a stylus enabling Ganesha to write the epic Mahabharata for Vyasa. It also serves as a weapon enabling Ganesha to strike down the moon who laughed on seeing him ride a mouse. It also serves as a staff on which he rests his arms and meditates. Some people believe that the one-toothed Ganesha is a representation of Ardhanareshwara, the fused form of Shiva and Shakti. The side with one tooth represents Shiva, the spiritual reality. The side without the tooth represents Shakti, the material reality.

Devdutt Pattanaik

48

Rat

Early images of Ganesha, dated around 5th century AD, do not show him riding a rat. In fact, in early images, he is shown seated on a lion. This association with a rat comes from around 10th century AD. During this period, from the 5th to the 10th century AD, as the Puranas were becoming the most popular sacred document, and temple worship became more and more mainstream, Ganesha moved from being a fringe deity to a central deity. Ganesha Purana states that Rishi Parasara prayed to Ganesha as his hermitage was infested with rodents. Ganesha sat on the rats and since then Ganesha has been represented seated on a rat. In South Indian traditions it is said that the rat was once an elephant-faced demon who was defeated and domesticated by Ganesha. Ganesha pins down and rides a rodent variously identified as mouse, rat or bandicoot. This troublesome pest has over the centuries come to represent the unmanageable problems of life. Ganesha, as the provider of solutions, removes the pest of problems from our lives. The rat is also a fertility symbol. It reproduces rapidly. Its association with Ganesha is thus natural as Ganesha is associated with many other fertility symbols such as grass and serpent.

Devdutt Pattanaik

49

Snake

Ganesha nurtures the potential prosperity of the cosmos in his huge belly. He holds it all in with the serpent wrapped round his stomach. Some say that this naga is Adi Sesha, the serpent of time. Others say it is Kundalini, the serpent of cosmic potential. Just as the serpent sheds its old skin for the new, Ganesha ensures the renewal of wealth at periodic intervals. Once Ganesha ate so many sweets that his stomach burst open and all the food he had eaten tumbled out. So Ganesha used a serpent to tie his stomach and lock all the food in. The serpent thus symbolizes wealth retention and regeneration. It is interesting to note that Ganesha is associated with both predator (snake) and prey (rat). In his presence, the impossible happens, the snake and the rat live in harmony as friends. This can only happen in heaven. This makes the very being of Ganesha heavenly where the worst of enemies can become the best of friends. The snake has all its needs met and so has no desire to eat the rat and the rat in turn has no fear and feels no need to run away from the snake. The snake is sometimes worn like a sacred thread over the left shoulder and sometimes just held in the hand.

Devdutt Pattanaik

50

Peacock

In the Ganapatya tradition that was popular in Maharashtra between the 14th and 19th centuries, Ganesha is said to have taken birth on earth to destroy a demon called Sindhu who had become all powerful by swallowing the pot of Amrita, or nectar of immortality. While climbing a mango tree, Ganesha caused an egg to fall. It cracked and out came a peacock. Riding this peacock, Ganesha fought Sindhu, cut open his stomach, removed the pot of Amrita, and managed to kill him. Having fulfilled his purpose on earth, Ganesha gave his peacock to his brother Kartikeya who is more commonly associated with a peacock. During Ganesha Chaturthi, in areas in and around Mumbai and Pune, the crowds shout, "Ganpati Bappa Moraya, Pudhchya Varshi loukar ya," which translates, "Oh Ganesha come soon next year." The word Morya refers to Moreshwar, one of the main Ganesha temples in Maharashtra, where Ganesha is associated with a Mor or peacock. Perhaps the peacock represents the joy of nature when rain arrives. Thus when people call out to Ganesha to come soon the next year, they are perhaps also hoping for the return of the monsoon which heralds the dance of the peacock.

Devdutt Pattanaik

51

Modaka

Ganesha is fond of a particular sweet called Modaka. Modaka is a steamed dumpling made of rice flour dough containing jaggery and coconut and sesame. The shape and constituent of Modaka is very significant. It looks like a bag of money, similar to one carried by Kuber, treasurer of the gods. Thus is it a symbol of wealth, and all the sweet pleasures that wealth gives man. It is also shaped like an upward pointing triangle, which, in Tantrik art, represents spiritual reality, in contrast to the downward pointing triangle which represents material reality. Thus the Modaka has the aesthetics and flavor of material reality but the geometry of spiritual reality.

Part VI
Temples

Devdutt Pattanaik

52

Rock Fort

Perched atop one of the oldest rocks in the world (three billion years old according to geologists), 83 meters high, this temple in Tamil Nadu is also one of the oldest temples in India, dating back to a time as early as the 10th century AD, housing both Ganesha, locally known as Pillaiyar and his father, Shiva, locally known as Thayumana-swamy. From this temple one has a bird's eye view of the city of Trichy, Srirangam and the rivers Kaveri and Kollidam. Ganesha is rooted to this spot as Vibhishana struck him on the head at this point atop the hill. Vibhishana, brother of Ravana, was furious because Ganesha had tricked him into placing the image of Ranganatha, given to him by Ram of Ayodhya, on the ground, at Srirangam, before he had reached Lanka. Ganesha had taken the form of a cowherd to dupe Vibhishana. On recognizing the true identity of the cowherd whom he had struck Vibhishana apologized, established the temple and offered prayers to Pillaiyar. The temple also houses Shiva who local legend says took the form of a midwife and came to the rescue of a woman in labor who was all alone at home, hence the name, Thayumana-swamy, he who acted as a mother. This temple was first patronized by the Pallavas and it reached its final form under the Nayakas of Madurai during the Vijaynagar era. Later the British, during the Carnatic wars, fortified the temple giving it the name Rock fort temple.

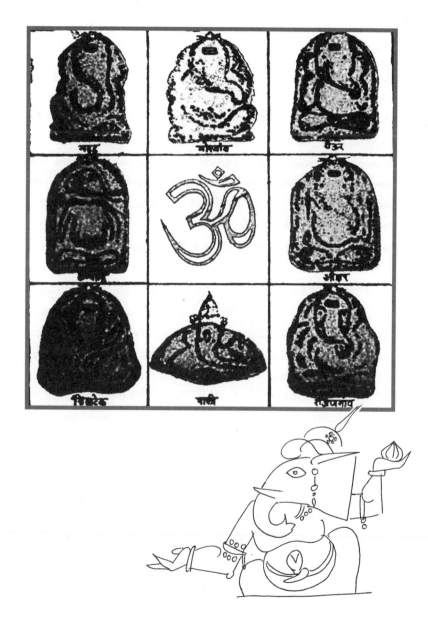

Devdutt Pattanaik

53

Ashtavinayak

These are a set of eight Ganesha shrines in Maharashtra that form a set of temples to be visited in a predetermined order to complete a pilgrimage. Each image is said to be swayambhu, meaning created not by man but by nature, and that makes them extremely sacred. The first and most important of these shrines is the Moreshwar temple at Morgaon, where Ganesha, mounted on a Mor or peacock, is said to have killed a demon called Sindhu. This is followed by a visit to Siddhivinayak of Siddhatek, Ballaleshwar of Pali, Varadavinayak of Mahad, Chintamani of Theur, Girijatmaj of Lenyadri, then Vighnahar of Ozar and finally MahaGanesha of Ranjangaon. The pilgrimage is supposed to end with a revisit to Moreshwar of Morgaon. In all these temples, Ganesha's trunk is towards his left side except in Siddhivinayak temple of Siddhatek where it is towards the right, making this the most fierce ascetic form of the eight Ganeshas on the pilgrim route.

Devdutt Pattanaik

54

Puri Elephant

The temple at Puri, in the state of Orissa, houses the images of Krishna as Jagannatha, lord of the world, his little sister, Subhadra and his elder brother, Balabhadra. Every year, at the height of summer, the deities bathe in the open. This is the great Snana-yatra that is witnessed by hundreds of devotees. Many centuries ago, a scholar called Ganpati Bhatta paid a visit to the court of the king of Puri. The king invited him to see the Snana yatra but the scholar declined stating that he refused to worship any god except Ganesha. The king insisted and not wanting to upset the royal patron, the scholar very reluctantly went to see the bathing ceremony. To his astonishment, he was unable to see Krishna; in the place of Krishna was Ganesha. Even Balabhadra had taken the form of Ganesha. He realized that Jagannath who is Vishnu and Balabhadra who is a form of Shiva, in their compassion, had taken note of his wishes and taken the form of Ganesha. The scholar also realized that the differences between Ganesha and Vishnu and Shiva were all artificial and not divine. Since that day, during the bathing ceremony of Jagannath, priests place the mask of an elephant on the two brothers. This is the Hati-vesha or the elephant dress, when Krishna and Balarama become black and white elephants respectively, each a form of Ganesha.

Part VII

Festivals

Devdutt Pattanaik

55

Autumn

Ganesha, and his mother, Gauri, are worshipped twice in a year, once in spring and once in autumn, perhaps in response to the two agricultural seasons of India, rabi and kharif. For he is the fruit of the earth and she is the earth. Ganesh Chaturthi is celebrated on the fourth day of the waxing moon in the month of Bhadrapad after the rains when the earth is green. It marks the start of the festival season. Ganesha is worshipped over a ten day period. After this comes the Pitr Paksha when the ancestors are worshipped followed by the nine nights of Navaratri and the five days of Diwali when the Goddess is worshipped. During this Ganesha festival, an image of clay is brought into the house, worshipped every day, and finally immersed in water after one, three, five, seven or ten days. This festival is now a pan-Indian festival especially popular in Mumbai and Pune where Ganesha is worshiped both in public pandals and in thousands of households.

Devdutt Pattanaik

56

Spring

Ganesha Jayanti is celebrated on the fourth day of the waxing moon in the month of Magh. This occurs in spring. This worship is restricted to Maharashtra and certain parts of Uttar Pradesh. It is considered the birthday of Ganesha, though there are those who believe that Ganesha's birthday takes place in autumn after the rains. The festival involves worshipping the image of Ganesha that is eventually immersed in water. The image may be anthropomorphic and made of clay or simply an aniconic lump of turmeric (haldi) or red sandal-paste (raktachandan) on betel leaf. Offerings include sweets made using sesame (til).

Devdutt Pattanaik

57

Chaturthi

The fourth moon or chaturthi is associated with Ganesha. The fourth day of the waxing moon is called Vinayaki-chaturthi: worshipping Ganesha on this auspicious day brings success. The Vinayaki chaturthi which falls in the bright half of Bhadrapad, August-September, is most auspicious as it comes after the monsoons when the earth is green with new vegetation, like the Goddess draped in a green sari. The Vinayaki chaturthi which falls in the bright half of Magh, January-February, is also celebrated in some parts of India as Ganesha Jayanti. The fourth day of the waning moon is also sacred, a day when Ganesha needs to be worshipped to avert problems. This fourth day of the waning moon is known as Sankashti-chaturthi. Worshipping Ganesha on this inauspicious day (inauspicious because the moon is waning) averts disasters. People usually fast on this day till moonrise. If Sankashti-chaturthi falls on Tuesday it is called Angarika Chaturthi and is especially auspicious.

Devdutt Pattanaik

58

Pancha Ganesha

This is a contemporary 5-day festival celebrated from December 21st to 25th in the USA by Hindus living in America in order to create a festival that Hindu children can celebrate when all of America is celebrating either Christmas (Christian festival) or Hannukah (Jewish festival). Each day, the image is decorated with a particular color: yellow on the first day, then blue, then red, then green and finally orange. This festival has been spearheaded by the Himalayan Academy based in Hawaii, founded in 1970 by Satguru Sivaya Subramuniyaswami.

Part VIII

Rituals

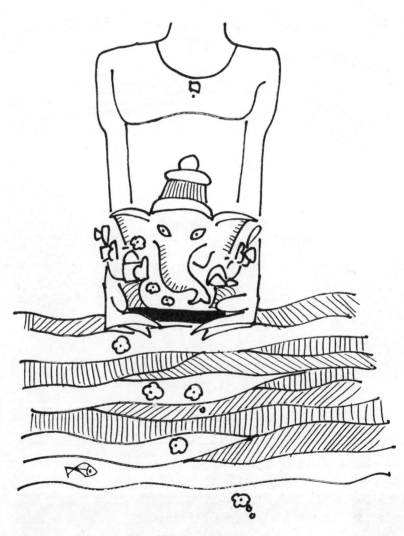

Devdutt Pattanaik

59

Cyclical

Ganesha idols are made using clay. Or he is represented symbolically by a lump of turmeric or red sandal paste (rakta-chandan) on a betel leaf. In this form, he is worshipped on Ganesh Jayanti or Ganesh Chaturthi. After the prayers are over, the image of Ganesha is dunked into a water body and dissolved. Thus the deity is created for some time, exists for some time and is destroyed eventually, only to return the next time it is time to worship him. This practice draws attention to the cyclical nature of life. Nothing is static in this universe. Everything changes. All things that go around, eventually come around. The seasons go and come, the tides flow and ebb, the moods rise and dip, the moon waxes and wanes and so too do fortunes and the quality of relationship undergo a change. Ganesha worship draws attention to the ever-changing ever-repeating nature of life. What dies, is reborn. In the Hindu scheme of things, death is not a full stop; it is a comma, to be followed by another life and another.

Devdutt Pattanaik

60

Two Gauris

During the ten-day Ganesha festival held in autumn in the West Indian state of Maharashtra, three days are dedicated to the arrival, worship and departure of Gauri, the mother of Ganesha. In many parts of the state, two female images are brought into the house. Both images look the same. One is called the elder Gauri or Jyestha and the other is called the younger Gauri or Kanishtha. One is poor, the other is wealthy. The two Gauris are identified as Parvati and Lakshmi, or as Ganga and Gauri. Perhaps they represent Gauri and her sakhi, or female companion, called Malini, who is mentioned in the 13th century manuscript Haracharitachintamani. Some are of the opinion that the two Gauris perhaps do not represent Ganesha's mother but represent instead, his wives.

Devdutt Pattanaik

61

No moon

Devotees of Ganesha avoid looking at the moon on the days that he is worshipped. This is because the moon incurred the wrath of Ganesha by mocking him for riding a tiny rat. The wrath was tinged with envy because Ganesha's unconventional form never got him the attention of women that came so easily to the handsome moon-god Chandra. Also, the moon is associated with Shiva who beheaded Ganesha and who competes with Ganesha for the attention of the Goddess Parvati. It is said that Krishna saw the moon on the Bhadrapad Vinayaka-chaturthi. As a result he was accused of stealing the sacred Syamantaka gem. He could absolve himself only after many misadventures.

Devdutt Pattanaik

62

Pillaiyar Suzhi

In Tamil Nadu, Pillaiyar Suzhi or Ganesha circle is drawn first before writing anything on paper. It is comprised of a circle, a curve, two lines and a dot. Perhaps in earlier times, when there was no paper, scribes used palm leaves to write on. Before they started writing, they checked the quality of the leaf by making a circle, a curve, a line and a dot. This came to symbolize Ganesha, the scribe who helped Vyasa write down the Mahabharata. Since then the Pillaiyar Suzhi is supposed to make things auspicious and bring good luck. In exams, students draw this symbol at the beginning of their answer paper in the hope that the exams go well. This Pillaiyar Suzhi in Tamil Nadu serves the same function as the mark of Shri in North India. Shri is also said to be another name for Ganesha. By writing his name in the beginning, one is heralding auspiciousness and ensuring absence of obstacles in any activity.

Devdutt Pattanaik

63

Hibiscus Flowers

In Hindu mythology, the Goddess who is Shakti exists both within and around us. Within us, she is the mind, the repository of our thoughts and feelings, our memories and imagination. Around us, she is the earth. Within or without, Shakti can be wild or tame. Wild, she is known as Kali. Domesticated, she is known as Gauri. Kali is the unbridled mind while Gauri is the disciplined mind. Kali is the forest, Gauri is the field. In iconography, Kali is naked with hair unbound while Gauri is dressed with hair bound with fragrant flowers. Ganesha is the son of Gauri, for maternity domesticates Kali. Shakti begs Shiva for a son; when Shiva refuses to give her one, she creates the son by herself. When Shiva beheads the child created by Shakti, Gauri threatens to return to her wild primal form, Kali, frightening Shiva who promises to resurrect Shakti's son. Thus the relationship between the Goddess and her son is a very intimate one. That is why the Hibiscus flower, which looks like a blood drenched womb is sacred to both Shakti and her son.

Devdutt Pattanaik

64

Blades of Grass

Offerings of blades of grass, known as Dhurva, form a critical ingredient of Ganesha worship. In Mumbai's Siddhi Vinayaka temple he is offered garlands of green grass and red hibiscus flowers. Rings of grass are worn on the finger while performing all Vedic rituals. This is supposed to purify the performer and prepare him for the ceremonies. Grass has the unique quality of growing back once it is plucked. It is resilient and can withstand water scarcity. It is supposed to possess this quality because it is believed that long ago, when the gods churned the ocean of milk, out came a pot containing Amrita, the nectar of immortality. This pot was placed on a bed of grass. This has given grass the ability to regenerate itself easily. Grass thus represents the power of renewal and regeneration. The same idea is represented by the snake around Ganesha's stomach. Together the two fertility symbols represent the human desire to replenish and revive all things that decay.

Devdutt Pattanaik

65

Vegetation

Vegetation plays an important role in Ganesha worship. His most famous festival takes place in autumn as the rains are waning and the earth is green. He is called the creator of eighteen medicinal plants. During Durga Puja in Bengal, in the last three days of the nine night festival of the goddess, nine herbs are tied together with a creeper (aparajita), decorated with a white sari with a red border, addressed as Kola-Bau, placed to the right of Ganesha and worshipped. These nine herbs, which includes turmeric, rice, banana, bilva, and ashoka, are associated with medicinal qualities and are visualized as goddesses. Ganesha as the son of Durga, the mother goddess, is thus associated with the produce of the land. He embodies the fruit of farming.

Devdutt Pattanaik

66

Bija Mantra

Every Hindu deity is represented using a sound. Ganesha is represented through the sound 'gan' ending with a distinct nasal twang. This sound has no meaning. It is not supposed to have meaning. It is believed to provoke vibrations that invoke Ganesha. A common chant prescribed by gurus to devotees is "Om Gan Ganeshaya Namaha". Devotees chant this 108 times. It is supposed to still the mind, calm the breath and lead one towards a direct communion with Ganesha.

67

Yantra

Every Hindu god is represented using a geometrical form. These are called Yantras. A basic Yantra principle is that circles represent nature while squares represent culture, dots and upward pointing triangles refer to spiritual reality while downward pointing triangles refer to material reality. All Yantras have some things in common. They are contained in a square with four T-shaped gates. This means a Bhupura or the worldly realm. Within is a circle, followed by 8 lotus petals emerging from another circle. Within this are patterns that differ from deity to deity. In a Ganesha yantra, the unique features within the final inner circle are:

- An upward pointing triangle
- An upward and a downward pointing triangle, crisscrossing, to create a six-pointed star
- A dot or bindu

An analysis shows that the image has more geometrical forms related to spiritual reality than material reality. This makes Ganesha a householder god with leanings towards asceticism.

Devdutt Pattanaik

68

Vishwaksena

Ganesha is invoked at the start of most Hindu rituals. However, this statement is not entirely true. Yes, Ganesha's name evokes auspiciousness and he removes all obstacles ensuring that the ritual will go forth without any hurdles. But in traditional Vaishnava (Vishnu-worshipping) communities, it is not Ganesha who is invoked at the start of a ritual. It is Vishwaksena, the herald and doorkeeper of Vishnu. In medieval times, there was much rivalry between the Shiva-worshipping (Shaiva) and the Vishnu-worshipping communities of India. Each one claimed that the supreme divine principle is best embodied in the form of the deity they worshipped. The rivalry was intense and sometimes violent. Naturally, Vaishanvas shied away from invoking Ganesha as he became, over time, more associated with Shiva. Hence the stories of Parashurama and Balarama breaking his tusk. Hence the story of Krishna falling under the malefic influence of Ganesha when he saw the moon on Ganesha Chaturthi. And so in major Vaishnava shrines like that of Venkateshwara Tirupati Balaji, a Ganesha shrine is not part of the main temple complex. He is outside. To reconcile the discomfort for traditional Vaishnava practices with the growing popularity of Ganesha, Ganesha is sometimes identified as a member of Vishwaksena's army.

Part IX
Literature

Devdutt Pattanaik

69

Ganesha Purana

Puranas are texts that chronicle the tales and the methods of worship of deities enshrined in temples. These are more recent Hindu texts, very different in character from the early Hindu texts, the Vedas, where the cornerstone of attention was not a deity but a ritual called the yagna. Ganesha Purana is a later Purana and identifies itself as an Upa-Purana or a minor Purana. It is one of the two Puranas that are specific to Ganesha and therefore highly referred to by Ganapatyas, the worshippers of Ganesha. It is dated between 10th and 15th century AD. It has two portions. The first portion is the Upansana-khanda, that contains details on how to express devotion towards Ganesha. This portion contains the Ganesha Sahastranama that contains the 1000 names of Ganesha, often chanted in Ganesha temples. The second part of the Ganesha Purana is the Krida-khanda that narrates the tales of Ganesha. This portion describes his four avatars in each of the four yugas. It also contains the Ganesha Gita.

Devdutt Pattanaik

70

Mudgala Purana

Like the Ganesha Purana, the Mudgala Purana is a Purana devoted to Ganesha. It is also dated between 10th and 15th century AD and scholars are divided as to which of the two is older. It is also an Upa-Purana, or minor Purana, that seeks to establish Ganesha as the supreme deity. The fundamental difference between Ganesha Purana and Mudgala Purana is that Mudgala Purana describes eight incarnations of Ganesha as opposed to four, and these are rather different in form and content.

71

Ganesha Gita

Ganesha Gita is part of the Ganesha Purana. It is a discourse given by Gajanan, an avatar of Ganesha, to a king called Varenya. Most of the verses from Ganesha Gita are taken from the more popular Bhagavad Gita, the difference being here Ganesha, instead of Krishna, takes the form of the Supreme Being. Ganesha identifies himself as the creator, the sustainer and the destroyer of the universe. He is Svayambhu or self-created, hence God. He also declares that whenever social order (dharma) is threatened, he descends to set things right. He offers his devotees three paths to reach him: the path of intellectual introspection (gyan yoga), the path of passionate devotion (bhakti yoga), and the path of detached action (karma yoga).

Devdutt Pattanaik

72

Maha Ganesha Upanishad

In the early part of the 18th century emerged an Upanishad that identifies Ganesha as the supreme being. This is known as the Ganesha Atharvasirsha Upanishad. Its origin is traced to the Atharva Veda. Upanishads are philosophical speculations, the earliest of which were composed 800 years before Christ. Since then from time to time, they have been rewritten over the centuries by various authors. A text written in 1751 identifies 108 Upanishads, which include the Ganesha Upanishad. Upanishads identify the supreme divine principle that animates all things and gives intelligence to the world as Brahman. In the Ganesha Upanishad, this formless divine entity is given a form, that of Ganesha. He is said to be the supreme divine principle containing all the gods. He is identified with Brahma and Vishnu and Shiva and with other Devas such as the sun and the moon and the wind and the fire and the rain. It also associates Ganesha with the Muladhar Chakra or the lowermost chakra of Tantrik physiology located at the base of the spine. He is even identified with the supreme mantra, Om. This Upanishad was created and popularized in the 17th and the 18th century by followers of the Ganapatya cult in Maharashtra, probably Chitpavan Brahmins of Pune. Other Ganesha Upanishads written around the same time with similar themes are Ganeshapurvatapini Upanishad and Ganeshottaratapini Upanishad.

Devdutt Pattanaik

73

Meteoric Rise

Academicians are bewildered by the meteoric rise of Ganesha in Hinduism. Vedic literature refers to a Ganesha identified as a scholar and leader of men, but there are no descriptions or association with elephants. Sutra literature speaks of wild spirits known as Vinayakas. Indo Greek coins dating back to 200 AD show elephant-like images. In the 3rd century AD text, Yagnavalkya-smriti, there is one Vinayaka who is a vighna-karta, or obstacle creator, but is associated with Ambika, the mother-goddess, and is a village deity or grama devata. From the 5th century AD, images of elephant-headed deities start to appear as a guardian god or as a subsidiary god or a god accompanying the Nava-grahas or the Sapta-Matrikas. From the 7th century AD onwards, the Puranas start identifying Ganesha as the son of Shiva and Shakti. In 9th century, Adi Shankaracharya refers to Ganapatyas, the cult of Ganesha worshippers as a major sect of Hinduism, equating it with Shaivas, Vaishnavas, Shaktas and Sauras, worshippers of Shiva, Vishnu, Shakti and Surya. From the 10th century AD, independent temples of Ganesha start appearing; he is shown with more than two arms, and riding a rat. By the 12th century AD, Ganesha worship had spread to Burma, Tibet, Japan, Thailand, Indonesia and Cambodia. In the 13th century AD, Ganesha Purana exclusively narrates the tales of Ganesha's adventures and grace. In the 19th century, Ganesha Upanishad qualifies Ganesha to be Swayambhu or self-created God, whom all other deities of the Hindu pantheon worship.

Devdutt Pattanaik

74

Indus

In the brick cities of the Indus valley civilization, dated around 2500 BC, archaeologists have found seals with the image of elephants. The script of the Indus valley civilization has not been deciphered and people wonder if they were the same as the people who revered the Vedas or different. The Indus civilization spread itself over vast parts of North West India and modern Pakistan and dominated the subcontinent for at least a thousand years before it collapsed mysteriously, probably due to climate changes, or the arrival of hostile tribes. That this great civilization had elephants on its seals indicates that elephants once roamed as far as modern day Punjab and Sindh. These were dense forests once upon a time, through which flowed mighty rivers like the Indus and the Saraswati. Perhaps elephants were domesticated then. If not they were admired from afar, admired enough to become part of seals. Did admiration extend to worship? No one is sure. But there is speculation that the idea of venerating a deity with an elephant body, or head, may have originated that long ago.

Devdutt Pattanaik

75

Vedic Ganapati

Ganapati is a title that appears in the Rig Veda, the oldest and most sacred of the Hindu scriptures. By the most conservative estimate, Rig Veda was composed around 1500 BC, around the time the pyramids were being built in Egypt. Ganapati means the chief of the ganas. The word ganas has many meanings. It can mean a tribe, a community, or a committee. It can also mean followers or companions. It also refers to a specific sound composed of three syllables. Ganapati thus means a leader, as well as a master of sounds. (Ganapati means the same thing as Ganesha), but the title Ganesha is not found anywhere in Vedic literature. It is not even found in the epic Mahabharata, which reached its final form around 300 AD. In fact, the word Ganesha appears only in Puranic texts, which started being written 2000 years after the Rig Veda, around 500 AD. Thus the original Ganapati was not quite the elephant-headed Ganesha we know today; it was a highly revered idea associated with a wise leader or a great teacher.

Devdutt Pattanaik

76

Vinayaka of Sutra and Smriti

Manava-griha-sutra, a manual on household rituals written about 500 years before the birth of Christ, refers to a group of four trouble-making deities known as Vinayakas. These were wild forest spirits to be feared and appeased. In the Yagnavalkya-smriti, written 300 years after birth of Christ, refers to only one trouble-making god or vighna-karta known as Vinayaka. By this time, the wild spirit has become a village god or grama-devata. When Puranic literature began being composed from 8th century AD onwards, Vinayaka came to have an elephant-headed form, and was less malevolent and more benevolent. In the Vamana Purana composed around 12th century AD, the name Vinayaka is derived from the tale of Parvati creating a child without (vina) a man (nayaka). By this time, the vighna-karta or obstacle-creating Vinayaka of the earlier treatise has become the vighna-harta or obstacle-removing Vinayaka. But memory of the old, much feared Vinayaka, still remains in tales of Ganesha in other parts of the world. For example, in Tibetan Buddhism one finds images of elephant-headed trouble-making imps being crushed by the Bodhisattva, and in Nepalese Buddhism one hears tales of how Vinayaka was part of Mara's army that tried to disrupt Buddha's meditation and how the Tantrik master Odiyacharya overpowered the elephant-headed trouble-making Vinayaka.

Devdutt Pattanaik

77

Yakshas

Ancient Indians, especially those who did not follow the Vedic rituals, believed in a class of beings called Yakshas. These were fat misshapen deities who lived in forests, especially close to water bodies and guarded treasures. Kuber, king of Yakshas, built the fabulous city of Lanka in the south and then, after being driven out by his half-brother, Ravana, king of Rakshasas, took refuge with Shiva, in the north, and built another fabulous city known as Alaka. Yakshas came to be known as Shiva's followers or Ganas. Shiva's son, Vinayaka, became leader of the Yaksha-ganas, which is why he came to be known as Ganesha. This story indicates the merger of the ancient Yaksha cult with Hinduism. Ganesha is very much like a Yaksha: elephant-headed, pot-bellied, and dwarfish. Worshipping him brought good luck and fortune. Kuber holds in his hand a pouch of money. The shape of the pouch very much resembles the modaka or the pyramidal sweet that Ganesha loves. Kuber's pet animal looks very much like Ganesha's rat. But it is not a rat; it is a mongoose which spits gems. There are temple images which show Ganesha and Kuber on either side of Lakshmi, goddess of wealth, indicating the close association of Ganesha with fertility and fortune.

Devdutt Pattanaik

78

Indo-Greeks

Following Alexander's invasion in 326 BC, many Indo-Greeks settled in India. Major contact was established between India and Greece during the reign of the Mauryas that followed. In this period, one comes across many Indo-Greek coins with elephant images or elephant-like symbols, leading many to speculate that Ganesha's form was inspired by the Greeks. One coin of Eukratides (2nd century BC), has the words 'nagara devata' or city-god written in the Karoshti script and shows Zeus seated with an elephant. The Greeks had conquered Egypt before they came to India and Egypt was known to have animal-headed deities like the falcon-headed Horus and the ibis-headed Thoth or the jackal-headed Anubis. Perhaps from here came the idea of an elephant-headed Ganesha for before the arrival of the Greeks, Indians did not have animal-faced deities. In fact, until the arrival of the Greeks, Indians did not have images of deities. Deities were ideas to be invoked through hymns or mantras. Idol worship was perhaps introduced to India by the Indo-Greeks. With the rise of the Roman Empire, trade routes were established with Rome. One Roman deity with whom Ganesha has much in common is the god Janus, after whom the month of January has been named. Both Janus and Ganesha are associated with thresholds and obstacles and change. Whether or not Greek or Roman or Egyptian gods influenced Indian thought, and the idea of Ganesha, remains a matter of speculation.

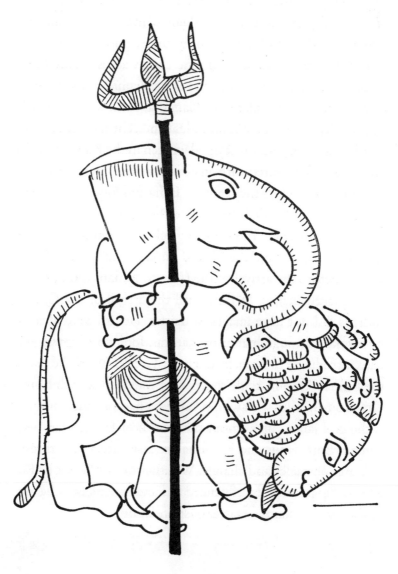

Devdutt Pattanaik

79

Hastimukha

Scriptures composed after the Rig Veda invoke deities with elephant attributes. These include Hastimukha, he who has the head of an elephant; Vakratunda, he who has a curved mouth or trunk; Dantin, he who has great teeth or tusks; and Lambodara, he who has a huge belly. In the south, the word Pillayar referred to a young one of an elephant, as well as an elephant-headed deity. The association of the elephant with Ganesha and Vinayaka occurred in the later phase of Hinduism, from around 5th century AD onwards. In the early phase, Hindus performed yagna, a ritual that involved invoking abstract deities by chanting hymns and making offerings into fire. But this old ritual appealed more to the elite and less to the masses. It gradually gave way to a new simpler ritual called puja, which involved praying to deities with animal, plant or human form with offerings of flowers, fruits, cloth and incense. As Hindus moved from yagna to puja, the abstract Ganesha and the malevolent Vinayaka became the more tangible, accessible and benevolent elephant-headed pot-bellied Ganesha.

Devdutt Pattanaik

80

Ganapatya

In the 8th century AD, the great Vedanta scholar, Shankar-Acharya, observed that Hindus across the land could be classified into five groups depending on the main deity they worshipped. These were the worshippers of Shiva, Vishnu, Shakti, Surya and Ganesha. Each of these groups saw their respective deities as the embodiments of all Vedic and Tantrik principles. They were further divided into six groups. The high point of Ganapatyas was reached around 10th century with the building of many Ganesha temples, the largest of which is the Ucchi Pillayar Koil (the Columns Hall of a Thousand Pillars), on the Rock Fort of Tiruchirapalli in Tamil Nadu. Around the 13th century CE, followers of the Ganapatya sect added two new chronicles (Upa puranas) to the vast repository of post-Vedic Hindu scriptures, namely Ganesha Purana and Mudgala Purana, which described the beliefs and customs of the Ganapatyas and many new tales of Ganesha. Later, the sect was popularized by Morya Gosavi who lived somewhere near Pune in Western India between the 14th and 17th centuries. Sect marks for the Ganapatyas included a red circle on the forehead, or the brands of an elephant face and tusk on the shoulders. Over time, the worship of Ganesha mingled and merged with the worship of Shiva and Shakti. His images were an essential component of Shiva and Shakti temples. Ganapatyas could not be distinguished from Shaivas and Shaktas.

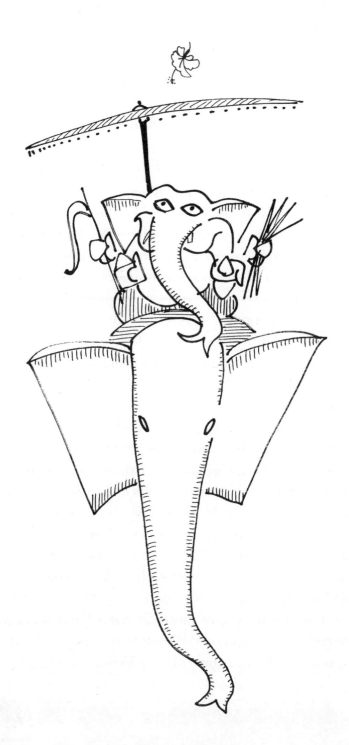

Devdutt Pattanaik

81

Tamil and Sri Lanka

In Tamil Nadu, Ganesha is called Pillaiyar. The story goes that when Shakti saw her son for the first time with an elephant head she said, "Pillai yaar?" or "Who is this little one?" From this came the name Pillaiyar. The word Pillai also refers to a baby elephant; it's a term of endearment. Pillaiyar falls within the Shaiva traditions of Tamil Nadu. No music concert begins without an invocation to Pillaiyar. Stories of Pillaiyar spread from Tamil Nadu to Sri Lanka. Amongst the Tamils of Sri Lanka, the story goes that Uma, wife of Shiva, wanted to bathe in a pond and so created a boy from a plant and ordered him to guard her clothes while she bathed. Shiva's companions told Shiva that a boy was standing by the pond where Uma was bathing. Assuming that the boy was planning to molest his wife, Shiva attacked the boy and cut his head off. Uma began to cry and explained what really happened. "If you resurrect this boy for me, I will give you seven boys, who will be your sons." Shiva then cut off the head of an elephant and resurrected the beheaded boy who became known as Vinayaka. Uma then created seven more boys. Shiva embraced them. But he could embrace only six, as the seventh one ran away. The six boys became one – the warrior god, Muruga, who has six heads. Thus, Shiva and Uma came to have two sons, Vinayaka and Muruga.

82

Morya

Morya Gosavi is perhaps one of the foremost leaders of the Ganapatya cult that popularized the worship of Ganesha as the embodiment of the supreme divine principle across India. Information about him is scant and scattered. He lived somewhere between the 14th and the 17th century and was closely associated with the temple at Moregaon. His tomb is located at Chinchwad, not far from Moregaon. He was born after his parents prayed to the Ganesha of Moregaon known as Moreshwar, hence the name Morya. Later, Morya moved from Moregaon to Chinchwad where his tomb stands till today. There are many stories why Morya shifted to Chinchwad. Some say he moved there to avoid the crowds at Moregaon and others say he moved there after marriage. He traveled to Moregaon regularly until he was too old to do so and so Ganesha appeared in Chinchwad too. While other saints patronized other deities, like Vithoba of Pandharpur, along with Ganesha, Morya Gosavi was exclusive in his devotion. It is in memory of Morya and his favorite deity, Moreshwar of Moregoan, that even today devotes address the Ganesha of Mumbai and Pune region as "Ganesha Bappa Morya".

Devdutt Pattanaik

83

Maratha influence

The popularity of Ganesha in modern times can be traced to Ganesha becoming the personal deity of the Maratha community that dominated the history of India in the 18th and the 19th century. It all started in the 13th century with Dnyaneshwar, a young ascetic who translated the Bhagwad Gita for the first time into Marathi, the language of the common man, despite virulent opposition from the Brahmin elite. In his writings, Dnyaneshwar said Ganesha's form was the visual equivalent of the mystical chant, 'Om'. Dnyaneshwar ignited the bhakti movement in Maharashtra known as 'Maharashtra Dharma'. Following him, many local saints such as Namdev and Ramdas invoked Ganesha in their songs. Morya Gosavi played a key role in making Ganesha a pivotal figure of the bhakti movement. Thanks to all these activities, Ganesha, until then a village god, came to the forefront of the devotional movement. He was the god of the people. The Brahmin community of Maharashtra, through their writings which included the Ganesha Purana and the Ganesha Upanishads, formalized the elevation of Ganesha from village god to embodiment of supreme divine principles. When the Peshwas came to be heading the Maratha Confederacy in the 18th century, they made Ganesha their personal deity. The Maratha confederacy, headed by the Peshwas, exerted its political influence across India from Delhi in the north to Madurai in the south. They patronized the worship of Ganesha wherever they went ensuring his popularity across the land.

Devdutt Pattanaik

84

Tilak

Until 1893, Ganesh Chaturthi, the great festival of Ganesha in the post-monsoon season was a private affair, usually performed within orthodox Brahmin households. In 1893, Balgangadhar Tilak, one of the earliest leaders of India's freedom struggle, turned it into a public festival. He did this in Pune with the intention of getting people together. There was no other reason for the elite Brahmin community to mingle with the non-Brahmin community. Tilak felt that a festival of this nature organized around the 'god of everyone' would get people to break out of the ghetto mentality and create a larger community. Tilak was a social reformer who introduced the idea of Swaraj or self-rule to the Indian National Movement. He was a visionary and realized that if India had to thrive, Indians had to overthrow the British and rule India by themselves. But for this to happen, people had to move out of caste and class confines and become a single people. Since political gatherings were frowned upon by the British, he came up with the idea of a public religious festival that people could organize. The community participation facilitated intellectual discussion, poetry recitations, music concerts, and performance of plays. Though religious and cultural in spirit, it played a key role in generating community spirit and was a precursor to future political gatherings.

Part XI

Spread

Devdutt Pattanaik

85

Nepal

In Nepal, Ganesha is worshipped by Hindus and Buddhists. A unique feature in Nepal is the worship of the Tantrik Ganesha known as Heramba. Heramba has five heads, ten arms and usually rides a lion. He is usually accompanied by his shakti, seated on his lap and receives blood sacrifices. This form is quite different from the gentle beatific form of Ganesha we commonly know. Nepal's Ganesha stands at the threshold of Vedic and Tantrik beliefs. It retains memory of the old Vinayaka, feared deity of the Shruti and Smriti traditions before becoming the much-adored deity of the Puranic tradition. In Nepal, there is a folk legend that when a girl realized that the beautiful man who had made her pregnant was actually a Bhairava known as Pachali Bhairava, with long fangs, matted hair and bulging eyes, she ran away in horror and delivered a baby prematurely, whom she abandoned. This child grew up to be the elephant-headed god of good fortune. Originally, he was part of the army of Mara, god of desire, who tried to disrupt Buddha's meditation. He even tried to disturb the practices of Odiyacharya, the Tantrik master, who overpowered him and pulled out one of his tusks. Ganesha surrendered to him and was admitted to the ranks of Buddhist deities who bring good fortune.

Devdutt Pattanaik

86

Tibet

Buddhism spread to Tibet after the kings there married Buddhist princesses from China and Nepal in the 7th century CE and as Buddhist scholars from India, like Padmasambhava, were invited there in the 8th century CE. The Buddhism that spread to Tibet was known as Mahayana Buddhism. It involved besides meditation and contemplation, the ritual worship of many Tantrik deities, amongst them Ganesha, better known in Tibetan Buddhism as Vinayaka. Ganesha of Tibet has two forms: one benevolent and another malevolent. In the benevolent form, Ganesha is the remover of the obstacles. In the malevolent form, he is the creator of obstacles. In the benevolent form, he looks very much like the images of Ganesha found in Bengal, white elephant head and red human body. He dances and is known as Maha-Rakta-Gana-Pati, the great blood-soaked leader of the Ganas. This form is said to be an aspect of the Bodhisattva Avatilokeshwara, who embodies the compassion of all Buddhas. In his more malevolent form, Ganesha is trampled by Maha-Kala, the Tantrik Buddhist form of Shiva, who represents all-devouring time. This form reminds one of the image of Shiva as Gajantaka, when Shiva flays alive the elephant-demon, Gaja-Asura, and dances on his head.

Devdutt Pattanaik

87

Mongolia

The worship of Ganesha spread along with Buddhism across Central Asia as far as Mongolia through the Silk Route and via Tibet. Images of Ganesha have been found in bronze, on paper and on wall frescoes. Sometimes Ganesha is represented as a powerful deity, usually two-armed, without pot-belly or rat vehicle, indicating that the transmission out of India took place before 10th century AD. According to a Mongol legend, derived from Tibetan legend, Ganesha raised the father of P'ags-pa, the Sakya Heirarch, with his trunk to Mount Meru and showed him the land of Mongolia and told him that his son would be its ruler. So it came to pass.

Devdutt Pattanaik

88

Burma

In Burma, Ganesha worship spread around 10th century AD. He is known as Mahapienne (Sanskrit Mahavinayaka) meaning Great Delight and he is one of the Nats (Sankrit Nathas) who are supernatural spirits guarding the Pagodas. Like other Nats, when propitiated, he protects people from calamities. The story goes that Indra, king of the gods, and Brahma, father of the gods, had a great argument on the number of days that should compose a week. Irritated by Brahma's intransigence, Indra cut his head off and then ordered the astrologer to replace it with the head of an elephant. Before this transformation, Brahma had a red and angry face. After the transformation, he had a golden elephant head and a red body. He seemed happier and was more benevolent and kind. He became less cantankerous and more helpful. The story is a reminder of Ganesha's transformation from the old trouble making vighna-karta to the later trouble-averting vighna-harta. He is shown with a rat, but sometimes is associated with many aquatic creatures like fish, tortoise and crocodile, indicating that he is also associated with fertility.

Devdutt Pattanaik

89

South East Asia

Around the 10th century CE, Indians traded with the Malay Archipelago which resulted in the spread of many Hindu customs, beliefs, tales and deities to these areas including Indonesia, Cambodia and Thailand. In Indonesia, he is shown sitting or standing, never dancing, usually with two hands, and significantly without a rat or any other animal vehicle, and often with skulls, indicating a Tantrik association. In Bali, he is shown with two tusks (not one), with two hands, holding a book, with no rat, and is invoked as a god and holy spirit to remove obstacles. In Cambodia too, Ganesha has only two arms, and significantly, he is not shown with a pot belly, or a rat, and in his hand, he holds Vishnu symbols like a wheel and a conch-shell. In Thailand, Ganesha is Phra Phikanet (Vighnesh) and Phra Phikhanesawora (Vighneshwara). He is worshipped with motaka, the Thai variant of modaka, when business is good but his image is turned upside down when business is bad. Unlike the Hindu worship of Ganesha, which is based on devotion, the Thai worship is more ritualistic suggesting that the Hinduism that spread to South East Asia was the pre-bhakti form of Hinduism, based more on ritual and less on emotion.

90

Japan

As Buddhism reached Japan via China around the 8th century CE, so did the worship of Ganesha thanks to the efforts of one Kobo Daishi. Ganesha did not have a significant impact in China; but he did appeal to some sections of Japanese society, especially the followers of the Shingon sect of Japanese Buddhism. Ganesha is a minor Buddhist deity worshipped as a single god known as Ganabachi (Ganesha) or Binayaka-ten (Vinayaka) and more popularly as the twin-god, Sho-ten or Kangi-ten. He is a very powerful god who brings happiness and bliss by removing obstacles. But the image of this deity, especially the twin images, is often not shown to the public; it is kept secret behind locked doors of the shrine. This may have something to do with the sexual nature of Kangi-ten's imagery; he is represented in dual form, two elephant-headed beings, one male and one female, neither with a pot belly, in an intimate embrace, suggesting Tantrik roots. Worshipped by traders seeking prosperity and young people seeking love, Kangi-ten is offered radish and sweet bliss-buns, a kind of Japanese modaka. The radish is raw while the buns are cooked; the radish is phallic while the bun is womb-like; thus the two complement each other as men complement women. The offerings, like the dual imagery of Kangi-ten, celebrate fertility and material well being.

Part XII

Wisdom

Devdutt Pattanaik

91

Kathenotheism

When Max Mueller, the 19th century German scholar, began translating the Vedas, he wondered if Hindus were monotheistic or polytheistic, did they believe in one god like the Christians and Muslims did or in many gods like the ancient Greeks and Egyptians did. For Max Mueller, monotheism was superior to polytheism, an indicator of cultural evolution. To explain Hinduism, he came up with the term, henotheism, meaning worship of one god while not denying the existence of other gods. He then found there were two varieties of henotheism – there was monolatry, worship of one god only to the exclusion of other gods, and then there was kathenotheism, meaning worshipping one god at a time. Ganapatyas followed monolatry; they worshipped Ganesha exclusively ignoring all other manifestation of the divine. But most Hindus follow kathenotheism; they worship Ganesha and all other forms of the divine, one at a time. At the time of worship, the object of adoration, whether Ganesha or any other deity, becomes the embodiment of the supreme divine principle.

Devdutt Pattanaik

92

Shankhya and Yoga

Ganesha's image can be seen in two ways. One way is to look at the parts – elephant head and human body. Another way is to look at the whole – a deity. The act of analysis where one focuses on the parts is called Shankhya. The act of synthesis where one focuses on the whole is called Yoga. The Veda says that human consciousness awakened with an act of splitting – spiritual reality broke off from material reality and began contemplating on it. This split is the primal split, when man could separate himself from the rest of the world. He could say, "I am this, but I am not that." Spiritual journey is the process of synthesis, of integration, when he can say, "I am this and I am that too." That process of integration involves expansion of consciousness, a process of merging our individual self with the rest there is. This process is called Yoga. It begins with Shankhya: recognizing what one actually is and what one actually is not. In other words beheading ourselves, recognizing that we are not our wealth, our families, our achievements, our bodies or even our minds. This will effortlessly lead us to Yoga: recognizing that ultimately we are all the same thing. In other words, Yoga will cause us to place an elephant head on our severed neck. Note, not a human head but an elephant head, for there will always be that rupture between material reality and spiritual reality.

Devdutt Pattanaik

93

Muladhara

Tantrik schools believe that the Goddess resides in our body at the base of our spine in the form of a coiled serpent called Kundalini. She seeks union with Shiva who resides on top of the skull. This is, for many, an allegory for arousing our consciousness so that we discover the soul. During this journey, we get many insights into the nature of our being and the world around us. With each insight we destroy our prejudices and have a better view of the world as it is. This arousal of Kundalini can be done through various Tantrik practices which includes chanting of hymns (Mantra), performing breathing exercises (Pranayama), performing various rituals which includes consumption of Alcohol (Mada), consumption of fish (Matsya) and meat (Mamsa), worship of special diagrams (Mandalas) and performing ritual sex (Maithuna). As the Goddess rises through the spine, like an uncoiling serpent, she causes six flowers (Chakras) to bloom, until she unites with Shiva. These flowers are milestones as our consciousness expands to realize Shiva. The first of these flowers is called Muladhara and its resident deity, located at the base of the spine is Ganesha. Ganesha is the first deity who must be realized in the journey that will unite the Goddess Kundalini, who is Shakti, with Shiva. In other words, unless we discover the wisdom of Ganesha, and realize the thought behind his form, we cannot begin our journey of self-discovery.

Devdutt Pattanaik

94

Liminal

What is Ganesha's form? Human or animal? This or that? Or both? Or neither? Sometimes, the truth does not exist here or there, but it exists in the in-between spaces. This is the threshold that connects the inner and the outer. This space is the called the liminal space, a space that is amorphous, shape-shifting, a bit of this and a bit of that. Ganesha is a liminal god, who connects two apparently opposing realities. Thus he connects Shiva, who is the transcendent formless spiritual reality with Shakti, who is the imminent tangible material reality. He is divinity within, she is divinity without. He is the observer, she is observation. He is thought, she is form. Ganesha connects the two, hence he is this and that, man and animal, fire and water. He is worshipped by the hermits who renounce the world as well as by householders who enjoy the world. That is why his image is often seen on thresholds of temples, not as a guardian but as the embodiment of the threshold itself, enabling all to move from here to there.

Devdutt Pattanaik

95

Tantrik or Vedic

The Ganapatyas could be divided into various groups, each one worshipping a separate form of Ganesha. There are the gentle forms, shown holding sweets, that are worshipped to remove obstacles. Then there are the more ferocious forms, often shown with a third eye and with a female deity or shakti on their lap. The gentle forms are called Vedic Ganeshas while the ferocious forms are called Tantrik Ganeshas. Vedic Ganeshas are either childlike or regal while the Tantrik Ganeshas are more aggressive, even sexual. Vedic Ganeshas are typically more yellow and golden while Tantrik Ganeshas are red and blue or black. Vedic Ganeshas usually show a broken tusk while this may not be seen in Tantrik Ganeshas. Vedic Ganeshas typically show the elephant trunk of the deity moving towards the heart while Tantrik Ganeshas typically show the elephant trunk of the deity moving away from the heart. Vedic Ganeshas are typically shown with one head while Tantrik Ganeshas often sport many heads – the former seeks to comfort the devotee while the latter leaves the devotee awestruck. Vedic Ganeshas are usually kept inside the house while Tantrik Ganeshas are usually kept in temples. Vedic Ganeshas became popular in India while Tantrik Ganeshas spread to Nepal and thence to Tibet and even Japan. The fundamental difference between Vedic doctrines and Tantrik doctrines is that the former looks at the material world as a delusion or maya while Tantra looks at the material world as power or shakti.

Devdutt Pattanaik

96

Omkar

Om is the primal mystical sound of Hinduism. Omkar means 'the syllable Om'. It is a verbal form of Brahman, the supreme divine principle. It is exclaimed at the start of most hymns, almost serving as a verbal herald that creates an aura of auspiciousness into which the rest of the hymn can follow. It is a humming nasal sound that many believe was inspired by the lowing of cows, the most sacred animal for Hindus. Rishis believed it was the first sound that the cosmos produced when it moved from inertia into activity. Scriptures like the Mandukya Upanishad are devoted entirely to the explanation of this syllable. It is composed of three sounds – A, U and M which represent creation, preservation and destruction. So sacred is this sound, that it is celebrated in all religions that took shape in India, not just Hinduism, but also Jainism, Buddhism and Sikhism. Every deity is identified with Om. When Kartikeya rose in prominence as Muruga in Tamil Nadu, he became the only one who could reveal the meaning of Omkar to Brahma himself. For Ganesha devotees, the sound of Om is visually represented in the form of Ganesha. Dnyaneshwar said that Ganesha's feet were equal to the sound 'a', Ganesha's stomach was equal to 'u' and Ganesha's head was equal to 'm'. Thus, Ganesha in totality is 'Aum' or 'Om'.

Devdutt Pattanaik

97

Swastika

The term Swastika, no thanks to Hitler, has become an ugly word in most parts of the world. It is tragic how dark events that happened over two decades ago make people forget a radiant heritage which is over two thousand years old. For two thousand years, or may be more, Swastika has been a symbol of auspiciousness and good luck in India. It is derived from the phrase 'su-asti', which means 'let good things happen'. Swastika is a visual representation of the desire for prosperity and peace. The diagram refers to the four gates opening in four directions (north, south, east, west), the four types of living creatures (those that swim, those that fly, those that walk above the ground and those that creep below the ground), the four aims of life (dharma or ethics, artha or economics, kama or aesthetics, and moksha or spirituality). It can also represent the sun with its rays radiating outwards. For many worshippers of Ganesha, this is a symbolic representation of Ganesha. The four curves represent four parts of his body – the head, the hands, the stomach and the feet.

Devdutt Pattanaik

98

Shri

The word 'Shri' means material auspiciousness. It has to be contrasted with 'Om' which is a primal sound, less material, more mystical. Shri is associated with wealth, bounty and affluence. When a man marries a woman, he becomes Shriman, a man with access to Shri, and his wife becomes Srimati, a woman with access to Shri, for in the Hindu scheme of things a man and woman have rights to material pleasures and wealth only after marriage. Traditionally, the word Shri is written on top of certificates, contracts and key documents. The word Shri is seen on top of wedding cards even today. It heralds prosperity and joy and good luck. Shri is another name for Lakshmi, goddess of prosperity. However, in many parts of Maharashtra, Ganesha is identified as Shri. With his vast belly, he is the embodiment of auspiciousness.

Devdutt Pattanaik

99

In the Beginning

There are two principles in life: certainty and uncertainty. Certainty is about order, control, and predictability. It is a space where one feels safe, but it is also a space where there is no growth. Uncertainty is about chaos, lack of control and absence of any predictability. It is a space where one feels frightened, but it is also a space where there is growth as new things, both physical and psychological, are discovered. In the Upanishads, the word for divinity is Brahman derived from the root 'Br' which means 'to grow'. Only in the pursuit of growth does one discover divinity; that is the purpose of life. To grow, one has to step into the unknown. One has to step out of the familiar into the unfamiliar, from the comfort zone to the zone of discomfort. As one takes this step, one remembers Ganesha. He is the lord of obstacles – he is vighnakarta, who brings obstacles, and vighnaharta, who takes away obstacles. Both are good. When he presents obstacles and we strive to overpower them, we gain Saraswati. We grow intellectually and emotionally, become wiser and more mature. When he takes away obstacles and things move smoothly, we gain Lakshmi. We grow materially, we become rich and prosperous, and experience joy. Either way we come closer to the discovery of divinity. So we take his name at the beginning of all ventures in the hope that he ushers us towards whatever we deserve or whatever we desire, until finally, having explored material reality, his mother, Shakti, we realize spiritual reality, his father, Shiva.

Pillaiyar of Rock Fort as Ganesha
is addressed in South India

Acknowledgements

- Harpreet, beloved of Hara and Hari, for those wonderful photographs
- Geetanjali and the editorial team of Jaico, for helping with text
- Dhaivat, and his team, who designed the book with so much affection